RODEO

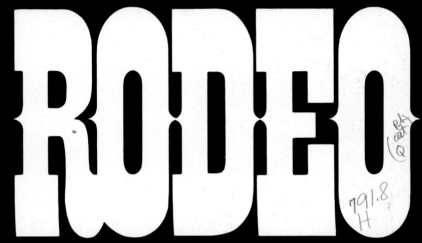

RODEO

by Douglas Kent Hall

BALLANTINE BOOKS · NEW YORK

To my mother,
and to Grandma:
she knew the old bronc riders...

And to the cowboys in this sport of sports—
my greatest respect and admiration

Why does he ride for his money
Why does he rope for short pay
He ain't gettin' nowhere
And he's losin' his share
He must've gone crazy out there.
—Mike Burton

INTRO-
DUCTION

Who knows where or when
o really began? There is a fine line between the point at which
t we now call rodeo stopped being a part of regular everyday
h work and the point at which it took on the status of sport and
rtainment. The change can't be pinpointed with any accuracy to a
in time or a specific place. Towns have tried. Caught up in fustian
ts of civic pride, and employing whatever turn of fact they can muster
a sketchy Western history, towns have laid claim to the distinction of
g staged the first rodeo. Towns in Texas, Arizona, Colorado—towns all
the West—still insist that on one distant Fourth of July the sport of rodeo
born on their town square, right out in front of the courthouse, across
the hotel, kitty-corner to the saloon one way and to the barbershop the

other way. These stories of what it was like back there in the hazy confusion of the early days are generally embellished and cranked out by some chamber of commerce's publicity firm; they come complete with descriptions of buggies and wagons bunched together to barricade all the streets leading off the town square, of fabled horses with names like Cyclone, Grave Digger, Culdesac, and Monkey Wrench, horses that bucked and pitched and boiled up in a high twisting sunfish configuration, crashed through a hitching post, splintered a long lodgepole railing, and then went banging and clattering along a boardwalk until they finally burst through a set of doors and destroyed some saloon or store.

Not everyone will agree that rodeo started in town, in _any_ town. The most vehement argument comes from the old-time cowboys who say they were not only witnesses but also participants in the whole phenomenon. There are still a few old-timers left. You might find them sitting on a bank corner somewhere—if the town happens to be small enough; or maybe they'll be all stove-up and forgotten on the porch of an old folks' home, wasting, battered men whose leathery faces are shot through with fine red veins at the cheekbones and whose hands are scarred by ancient tracks where a twisted lariat burned away hard calluses and bit into the raw flesh. These old cowboys, jackknives honed on Carborundum and dressed down on a boot top, spend whole days idly whittling the past out of a piece of clear boxwood. Tell them what the towns say and the knives will stop. They'll snort a derisive little laugh and their eyes will leap with an eager spark: Towns be damned!

Rodeo started right out in the middle of nowhere, in the dirt and brush. No one can say when. Any man around in those times was lucky to know the year, let alone the day. If he even cared.

The old cowboys maintain that in the beginning it was nothing more or less than a contest between a horse and a man. Someone owned an outlaw bronc he claimed no man could ride; some cocky young cowboy stood back, sized up that famous horse, and said the hell he couldn't. The wager was made, the bronc snubbed down, saddled and mounted, and the matter was settled on the spot. Pure and simple.

That's how rodeo came to be, the old-timers insist, nodding firmly, rheumy eyes going just vacant enough to allow their minds to focus back on the time when they did or didn't ride whatever notorious horse it was they measured their ego against and pitted a month's pay on. Rodeo is that and nothing more, just a horse and a man.

The old-timers are probably right: There was a horse and a man. The towns, too, are right: It took an audience to transform it from just another facet of everyday cowboy work to a sport.

Still, it must have been more. Both the horse and the man had been around for thousands of years before there was anything that even vaguely resembled rodeo. It has been estimated, for instance, that Eohippus—or the dawn horse—appeared at least fifty million years ago; this creature, barely the size of a small dog, evolved into what science calls Mesohippus and Protohippus stages, growing larger and taking on more definite equine characteristics with each change, finally reaching the form of the modern horse about one million years ago. According to the best evidence we have from archeologists, man first hunted the horse as a source of food; then, some time during the last few thousand years, he domesticated the horse and started using him for such purposes as work and war. During this long time, it seems strange that the kind of man and horse that eventually produced rodeo could not have met; certainly not all those horses were docile and all the men passive.

Apparently, the answer lies in America, in the American West, in something that happened there. During its evolution in ancient times, the horse flourished on the American continent. For some reason—perhaps because of disease or famine—it perished entirely and did not reappear until the sixteenth century, when it was shipped over from Spain by Hernando Cortez. The horse the conquistadores brought to America was one the Spanish had bred specially for their purposes, crossing the fleet Arabians out of North Africa with heavier breeds brought down from the northern part of Europe. Those horses that were lost, run off, and then finally left to roam loose in Mexico and what was to become the southwestern United States grew into the stout-hearted mustang and the Indian pony. They developed a disposition never before known in the horse.

Something similar happened to the man. The West singled out a special kind of man, almost a separate breed, and gave him both a calling and a creed. Some people would say that the man too went wild. As wild as the horse. And maybe after his own fashion he did. However you look at it, the horse and the man had been transformed; they had become something they had never been before. The West can do that to horses and—especially—to men. It has and it will—not to every man, and not to the same degree. It singles them out and leaves its mark on them. It's enough to make them take the name of cowboy, enough to let them get into a game like rodeo.

What we call the West is not an area determined by the limits of elementary geography. That quality that could once make a man trade four walls and a family for a bedroll and a saddle won't come through the crisscross ribbons of concrete that bind up Dallas or Denver or Phoenix; nor can it be bought with a tract house in the suburbs of Tulsa or Reno. But if you stop for a moment just outside of Meeker or Gruver or Globe, you might begin to feel it, out on the edges of that wild country, still as potent as it ever was, still calling to that man.

The West has a distinctive look and smell and feel. There is about it an inexplicable sense of something big, something outsized and exaggerated—except it is also subtle, which is equally inexplicable. You might find it in something as simple as the way tall buffalo grass gradually gives way to sage, the sage to cactus, cactus to sand; or feel it in those dry chiseling winds that send tall clouds kiting across a sky as wide as Wyoming;

or see it in the thin comb of rain hanging on some distant horizon.

Whatever all this is and however it comes, the West will always appear to be "more," and "different." It's not exactly the sage, or the rain either. It goes deeper, beyond the soil, into the land itself. The West is restless and changeable. It has at its heart a kind of underlying purity which can recast life and hone it to a new edge. It did this with the Andalusian horse the Spaniards brought and left, and with the strange man we've come to call the cowboy.

The cowboy is an anomaly. **He is mythical, legendary, a twenty-four-carat original freak of human nature.** He was born full-grown in the West; it gave him his life and sent him out green to ride out his own history in a new and hostile land. Not even imagination has produced an equal to this hero wrought out of circumstance and necessity.

Cowboys came from anywhere (they still do), as though the West were some kind of gigantic magnet. They had names—real or made up—or no names. There was a place for the good man and the bad man—and the distinction between them was often difficult to make.

The cowboy image is studied and self-conscious. I recall an old photograph of one of the cowboys in my family, a posed shot of Grandma's brother. He is standing in the middle of a muddy street in Wheatland, Wyoming, some time after the turn of the century. The month is probably March, for there is a bit of late snow in the background and his horse still has a shaggy winter coat. The saddle he is about to climb into is the old type: high-dished cantle, generous swells to the fork, and a trim metal horn. He wears a huge Hoot Gibson hat, pushed back and raked to one side. His scarf seems large enough to serve as a tablecloth. He wears his vest open. His chaps are cut from long stringy angora. Forked onto his high, slant-heeled boots (I know the tops would be tall, with a surplus of fancy stitching and pictorial inlays) are spurs with mean-looking spiked rowels big enough to roll a wagon on.

The cowboy wanted to **own little more than he could wear or ride. He craved a special freedom; and once he had gained that freedom he was proud enough and jealous enough of it to guard it with his life one** moment and reckless enough to turn right around and risk it in the most foolish way the next moment. There was—and still is—so much haphazard perfection in the image of this man who suddenly seemed to appear full-blown to fill a need that even he was fascinated by his own kind. His lack of any viable model of what he should be and how he should look and his being given the free hand of improvisation, limited and directed only by the forces of his environment, left him to shape his own image as he saw fit. The image he finally chose, through trial and error, was so fabulous and inflated it assumed the proportions of myth.

Even after there were no more cattle trails and most ranges were cut gridwise with barbed-wire fences, there remained a man who had discovered a life he refused to let die. Not that he was suddenly out of work. It was just that any and all ranch work looked too much like ordinary dirt farming to be attractive to someone who wanted to really cowboy. Of course, openings could be found in the Wild West shows. Buffalo Bill had his; and there were others. They allowed a cowboy to indulge his image. But what that was and how he illustrated it had to fit someone else's pattern. So, finally, the Wild West show wouldn't cut it either. There was too much of the circus in it— and too much of the regular job.

Rodeo was something else. It started to come into its own in the early part of the century. The circuit was pretty sketchy. But it was loose, and included enough glory to keep a cowboy's life from getting dull. He could go and come as he pleased. He could ride and win. Rodeos took him back to where it all started: the animal, the man, the challenge, and the chance.

How this happens or why it happens to one man and not another is hard to say. It's like an infection that starts and spreads. A man wants to be a cowboy. He feels born to it, predestined. Charlie Siringo, in <u>A Texas Cowboy</u>, wrote: "In the spring of 1867, a cattle man by the name of Faldien...persuaded mother to let me go with him, and learn to run cattle. When she consented I was the happiest boy in the 'Settlement,' for my life long wish was about to be gratified." In <u>We Pointed Them North</u>, Teddy Blue Abbott, who was born in England and brought to a farm in Nebraska, relates that "...from '71 to '78 I was tending my father's cattle around Lincoln and growing up with the men who came from Texas with them. Those years were what made a cowboy of me. Nothing could have changed me after that." Phil Lyne, the 1971 and 1972 World Champion All-Around Cowboy, remembers roping his first calf at the age of four. Larry Mahan, six times the World Champion All-Around Cowboy, grew up on two acres in Oregon. But as he puts it, "My name was 'Cowboy' because I was the only kid with boots and a hat."

From Charlie Siringo to Larry Mahan and the younger men on the circuit, the ingredients for a cowboy have remained the same. Rodeo has inherited all that the Old West had to offer—the hardship, the exaggeration. What was once a tough life is even tougher today. The cowboy is no ordinary man, he never was. And, true to that tradition, rodeo is no ordinary sport.

BRITCHES

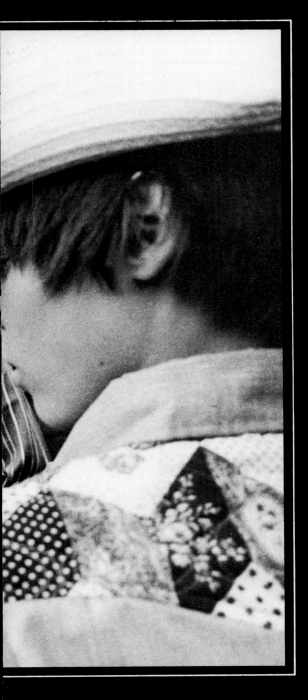

The only way to break into the cowboy life used to be the hard way. You just did it. You learned to ride by climbing on a horse. You learned to stick to a bucking bronc by climbing onto the wildest critters you could find so many times that common sense and what little bit of laconic advice was forthcoming from the sidelines either taught you how to stay there until the bucking stopped or told you that you'd better quit. Naturally, it was only the man with the desire and passion to be a cowboy who finally made it. The idea was simple: If you wanted it bad enough you'd get there. You didn't care about your body as long as it somehow came through all the crashes intact, but you did care about your pride.

Basically, none of that has changed with rodeo. Any kid can be a cowboy. From the point of view of practical experience, a kid raised on a ranch might have the best shot at it. But that doesn't always hold true. Cowboys today can come from Brooklyn or Chicago. In rodeo, it's ability and sheer determination and not background that make a cowboy.

One avenue open to an aspiring young cowboy is youth rodeo or junior rodeo. These rodeos for kids have been going on for years in conjunction with fairs and other functions sponsored by 4-H Clubs and schools. In 1961, the National Little Britches Rodeo Association was organized. Its purpose was to incorporate the junior rodeos around the country, standardize the events, and set down rules that would govern them. As is the case with all rodeo organizations, including Girls Rodeo, Little Britches consciously patterned itself closely along the guidelines set up by the Professional Rodeo Cowboys Association (PRCA), with the obvious goal in mind of making it possible for a young cowboy to come up through the ranks of Little Britches, move into collegiate rodeo, and then go on to professional rodeo.

Little Britches has done remarkably well. It now sanctions almost 100 rodeos per year throughout the United States in which nearly 14,000 contestants between the ages of 8 and 17 participate. The age span here is significant; and in an attempt to promote fair competition the young cowboys and cowgirls are separated into four classes: Junior Boys (8–13) and Senior Boys (14–17), with the same age divisions for Junior Girls and Senior Girls. Because of the age and size differences, coupled with the natural fierce competitive spirit of kids, there is a lot more preliminary rope-throwing and

14

swaggering and cautiously circumspect sizing up among the Little Britches than among the pro cowboys. It is especially evident in the Senior Boys division, where the degree of development between a "young" fourteen-year-old and an "old" seventeen-year-old is probably greater in terms of both mental and physical maturity than at any other period of growing up.

Little Britches is busy rodeo. For each of the four classes of competitors there are five events. This means that as many as twenty events, all different, all separate, can be featured at a single rodeo and (according to the bylaws set out in the Official Rule Book) no fewer than fourteen events can be featured even at a small rodeo. The result is that at a Little Britches rodeo there is twice as much action as at a regular professional rodeo, which normally has five events and sometimes six or seven. This much action can be confusing, especially in the big rodeos where at least one event is going on in the arena while another event is being held on the track.

The parents seem to be as enthusiastic about Little Britches as the kids. "You can't stop

them," said one mother. "Kids just seem to get all obsessed with rodeo. They want to ride anything that will buck, rope anything that will run—including cats and chickens. They chase everything you have on the place. And I guess it's good. They're going to do something anyway. You just hope it's something constructive. I feel personally that rodeo's a lot cleaner and better sport than something like football."

One man, whose son had just turned eight and was beginning in Little Britches, said he would help him go as far as he wanted in rodeo. "I think it'll give him something exciting and rewarding to do. I think it'll make him a better man and a better human being. It'll give

him a chance to discover whether or not this is what he wants. If it is he'll have the opportunity to learn to do it well. And if he discovers he can't do it, then he'll at least have the confidence of having tried, and that'll help him to go on to something else."

Most of the kids don't look at it the same way. In an interview conducted during the filming of The Great American Cowboy, Wade Hedger, 14, a Little Britches cowboy from Las Vegas, Nevada, summed it up as follows: "They don't have near as rank horses for us as they do at the professional rodeos. Those guys are professionals and we ain't. We're just a bunch of kids trying to ride and have fun." He was serious, however, about his own goal in rodeo. "It's a sport and I like it. I'd rather do this than smoke dope and stuff. I think it's a lot more fun, too; you get a lot more out of it. I'd say it's more fun to ride a bareback horse and get your arm broke than shoot speed and get killed or something like that. I'd just rather ride in rodeos."

The cowboy has probably been the subject of more hyperbole than any other breed of man, much of which he has been responsible for fostering and then encouraging. A close look at the Little Britches tells a lot about how it happened. In their own way, the kids are much more colorful than the pros. This has to do partly with an inadvertent and unintentional exaggeration when the kids try to imitate their idols with some shoddy makeshift gear. It comes through most clearly in cowboy costume. The kids want to look like the real thing so bad they overdo everything. Two years ago at the Cow Palace in San Francisco, Larry Mahan bought an Indian choker made of turquoise and shell. He might not have been the first cowboy to do it; but he tends to be noticed the most. Now the kids have picked up the fashion, wearing beads and bangles they wouldn't have dreamed of owning back in the days of Bill Linderman and Jim Shoulders.

A professional cowboy will take custom-made gear and then work fanatically to tailor it down until it is absolutely right for his body. The Little Britches cowboy tries to do the same. But it's impossible. In look and size, his body is going through its most rapid and most extreme change. His clothes always seem too big or too small. Often the silver belt buckle he's won somewhere is so huge it seems more like armor than a trophy. Either his chaps are dragging in the dirt or they are creeping up toward his knees. One pair I noticed at the Little Britches Finals Rodeo had twice been added onto at the bottom, each time with a slightly different color of leather.

I expected to see twisted cinches and latigo leathers and too much rosin and potential booby-trap riggings (all of which I did see at Little Britches rodeos); but what really surprised me was the individuality I saw in the young cowboys' hats. Out on the pro circuit, you don't see a lot of variation in hat styles or anything else; there are three or four basic creases, with a few—and very few—freakish innovations. But the kids' hats were fantastic. There was everything from huge droop-brimmed monstrosities almost big enough to double as tents to neat woven straw hats with perfect creases. An occasional crown would be adorned with a tiny silver emblem symbolic of the cowboy's particular event. Feathers and imitations of folded one-hundred-dollar bills were stuck in the bands; one kid even wore a tight little plastic bouquet he probably lifted from the table setting in some small-town café.

Naturally, the whole cowboy imitation went further than fashion and equipment. One of the most amazing things was how many of the kids were using snuff. That round tin of Skoal or Copenhagen you get used to seeing around rodeo seemed to be wearing a circle in a pocket of almost every pair of jeans. Snuff was the thing. Girls had it, and even a little boy who could hardly have been more than seven was dipping. Remembering my own bad day after trying a chew of Beechnut, a taste that can still cause me to shudder, I concluded that these kids must be a lot tougher than I ever was. Then, walking around the corner of a building, I caught sight of a boy vomiting up his guts while trying desperately to keep the stuff from staining his new cream-colored chaps. No, no different—or tougher either.

Still, whatever happens behind the chutes before the show, all the stall-walking and moon-posing and vain attempts at impressing one another, down in the chutes things get deadly serious for the Little Britches cowboys. As Larry Mahan will tell his rodeo school students: The animals don't know that this isn't a real rodeo, that it isn't a big-time rodeo. Because, in fact, it is real rodeo—complete with its share of bruises and broken bones and blood. A fact which is not lost on these cowboys. You can see them bat their eyes and stiffen just a little as they feel the first real surge of adrenalin start to flow. And gradually, as they get their rope pulled on a little bull, their saddle set on a bronc, or their rigging cinched over the withers of a nervous bareback horse, the total weight of what they are about to do comes down on them. The younger ones seem especially white-faced when they climb into the chute. Then, when they call for the gate to be opened and whatever fate that might offer, their cry is a piercing, strident shout.

In the arena, it is no longer a matter of age or size or know-how or anything else that seemed to count before. It's just exactly what the old-timer cowboys claimed: one man and one animal. Rodeo...

18

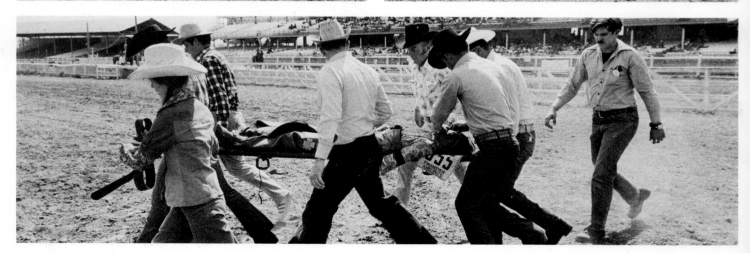

ROD

The old way—climbing on and bucking off, climbing on again and again until you figured it out—was not a bad way. Now, however, the old way is not considered the only way, or the best way either. A desirable alternative—which can hardly be considered an easy way—is to learn the basic cowboy skills at a short three- or four-day rodeo school where competent cowboys (usually men who have proved their superior abilities by competing for or winning world championships in their events) offer instruction on preliminary preparation, basic riding principles, and the more subtle points of technique developed and tested through their own experience and success in the arena.

I flew to Texas to observe a rodeo school conducted by Larry Mahan, easily one of the best-qualified instructors in the art of rodeo riding. Most of the students had shown up the day before the school was to start. They were hanging around the Steiner Ranch outside of Austin. They had come any way they could. Driving, taking the bus. One had hitched down from Montana—so he'd have enough cash to pay his school fee. A couple of buddies from the South somewhere came in an ancient pickup with a shell-like plywood camper on it. A kid from the East still had his first-class return ticket tucked in a neat shirt pocket.

The first morning, everyone was waiting for Mahan. They were excited and nervous, neither of which they wanted to let show. They concentrated on trying to maintain the elementary cowboy image they had learned in Little Britches and high school rodeo—detached, cool, tough, professional. It worked for a while, then it began to waste. They walked back and looked in at the bulls and horses. When they returned most of their bluff had given way to a kind of gnawing fear. The air was full of a feeling of reluctance, a feeling of wanting to prolong something they had all waited months to happen, something that had crept up too soon.

Mahan drove up in a moss-green Eldorado, just fast enough to shower the arena with dust and cause the young cowboys to brush at their clean shirts and cough. He was not late, but not early either. Rodeo has taught him a sense of timing.

Larry Mahan, the most successful cowboy in the history of rodeo, looks exactly the way he says a cowboy ought to look: smaller in stature than the average man, with a trim muscular build. He watches his diet with a relentlessness that would make a Weight Watcher squirm and stagger, and maintains a regular pattern of vigorous exercises in health spas and clubs wherever he travels.

He climbed the front of a chute gate, making them all look up at him and squint from under the brims of big hats into the already steamy Texas sun. "Boys," he told them, "there is no easy way into this game of rodeo...." He continued, painting a grim picture of what they could expect out of the sport if they decided to go on. Hardship, discomfort, pain. The school itself would be no picnic. By the time they were done that night most of them would be hurting. "So if you've come here expecting a summer camp and just want to horse around, that's fine. Tell me now and I'll stay off your butt. But you guys that are serious about it, you guys that really want to know about rodeo, when you screw up I'm going to be on your ass."

A little flurry of muffled laughter rose up and was immediately sucked away in apprehension. Already the chutes were banging and crashing as the cowboys who'd hired on as Larry's helpers loaded the first bucking horses.

Larry moved his leg to let a horse run past and kept on talking. "This is probably going to be one of the only times in the game of rodeo when you're going to have somebody like a coach who'll bother to cuss your ass out when you screw up. Because from this point on, you're going to be your own coach, your own trainer. And you're going to get out of it just what you put into it."

Another horse flashed past and the chute gate slammed shut. Then a horse bolted into the chute Mahan was sitting on and stood there quivering. Larry reached over and touched him. "These animals are dangerous. This is probably the toughest game in the world to break into because there's just no easy way. You can pitch a kid a football and tackle him easy. But you can't say to this horse or those bulls back there: 'Okay, take it easy, this kid's just beginning.' These animals don't know the difference between a student and a professional cowboy. They don't know the difference between a rodeo school and a regular rodeo. They're going to be serious every minute...and you'd better be too."

Mahan wasn't ready for them to mount out their first animals yet. First he wanted to go over the equipment each student had brought to the school. He had them all find a space along the fence and get everything laid out—riggings, saddles, ropes, reins, spurs, chaps. He started by telling them how important it was to have good equipment, the best they could possibly buy. And he pointed out that the best was not the fanciest or most expensive. He examined what each student had dug out of his rigging bag. He spared no one's feelings. "If you're going to try to ride with that thing," he told one kid about a sorry flimsy bareback rigging, "you're wasting your time."

His theory is that it's better to shame them than to have to haul them off to the hospital. Good equipment can be as instrumental in saving a cowboy's life and keeping him from injury as it can be in helping him make a winning ride.

Owning equipment of the highest quality is essential; but it isn't enough. Mahan told the students they needed to be so thoroughly familiar with their equipment they would finally find themselves thinking of it as a logical extension of their bodies. This applied to bull ropes, bareback riggings, bronc saddles, gloves; and it even extended to chaps and spurs. "You've got to work with your gear. Sit in that saddle, get your hand in that rigging, work on your bull rope. Get everything so it feels right. You've got to groove on this stuff. Instead of playing cards or twiddling your thumbs, start playing with your glove. Get so you can tie it in a hurry and it feels right. Then run your hand in your rigging, get the bind right, and start telling yourself, 'There's no possible way a horse can jerk this rigging out of my hand.'"

Once the equipment had been inspected and the students were on the chutes, setting their gear and getting ready to go out, Mahan really started working on their minds, on the mental aspect of rodeo. He feels this is as big a part of his teaching role as being able to criticize their actual riding. "Think positive," he shouted along

25

the chutes. "Tell yourself there is no such thing as a negative thought. Positive mental attitude. P...M...A!" he spelled it out. "You've got to have it if you're going to make it in this business. Write it down and stick it on your bedroom mirror. Rodeo is a constant job of working on your mind.and body. Remember that. It's not just going to happen. You can't just get on a bull and ride him. It's something you have to believe you can do. Every morning when you get out of bed you should have it fixed in your mind that you're going to be the guy to beat. And then go to it as if there's just no way you're not going to win. You've got to have that desire to win...."

Mahan is not alone in his attempts to make rodeo schools cerebral as well as physical. One cowboy-instructor has carried it one step further. Gary Leffew, the 1970 World Champion Bull Rider, suggests that his students spend twenty-one days changing their self-image and riding the bulls of the mind, or Zen Bull Riding. At one school he was conducting on his Santa Maria, California, ranch Leffew found himself confronting two students from the East who had a strong desire to ride bulls and the guts to go with it, but absolutely no natural talent or experience with animals. As he put it, "They couldn't even tell you the difference between a bull and a steer." They were bright kids who had both been to school, but he could see from the first moment they got down in the chute with their first bulls that they were not ready for it. So he made a deal with them. If they would go into the mountains and camp out and stay away from everything and work on changing their self-images and riding bulls in

their minds for twenty-one days he would allow them to come to his next school without paying tuition. The isolation and the mental thing Leffew had encountered in books about positive thinking; the discipline was something he'd learned in his reading about Zen. He'd proved them all out in his own life. His method of teaching the self-image change is to have the students choose a hero and pattern their lives after him.

One of the students going off to the mountains chose Donnie Gay. Remembering it makes Leffew smile: "Donnie Gay is one of the super bull riders of all time. He always had a kind of bebop attitude and he rode that way—a lot of showmanship and style. This one kid just programmed Donnie Gay into his mind the whole time he was up there. And when he came bebopping back for the June school, not only had his riding ability changed, but he looked like Donnie Gay. He walked like him; he acted like him. And he rode everything I had in the pens. You'd have thought it was Donnie Gay out there."

Part of building a student's self-image is showing the student how he looks when he rides. Mahan accomplished this with videotape. He had each ride shot with a portable camera. Immediately following the ride, he had the tape played back so the student could see it and have each of his moves and mistakes analyzed and criticized. Mahan had sufficient praise for the good things—if there happened to be any—and he got on the student's butt about the mistakes, especially those stupid mistakes that had to do mostly with what he called weakening, or being chicken-hearted.

All morning long, Larry Mahan kept shouting the words he knew could turn a serious student into a rodeo winner. "Be aggressive!" "Bear down!" "Try!" "Charge!" "Go, go, go!" He repeated himself over and over, as he warned he would. He let nothing pass. If a kid made a mistake, he jumped him about it. In Mahan's eyes there is only one way: do it right and win.

By noon, all the students fit into three groups. There were those who definitely would not make it in rodeo (and wouldn't even show up for the second day of school), those who might make it if they pulled themselves together and tried, and the one or two or three who might have more than a chance. Which class they would be in could be determined after the second or third time they climbed up over the chute gate.

It was a lot harder to get going after lunch. Mahan knew it, but he wasn't letting up—at least not on the best students. He praised them less and criticized them more. He saw what they could handle and then pushed them to the limit.

It isn't necessary to learn everything in the chute on actual horses and bulls. At some of Mahan's schools he uses a mechanical bronc, a rubber and steel creature set up with sprockets and chain drives run by an electric motor to simulate basic bucking patterns. For spurring practice he suggests a bail of hay. Gary Leffew

tells his bull riders to set up a barrel and work with it. "I recommend that every one of you guys build a barrel and practice on it, practice all the moves you're going to make on a bull. Practice them over and over so that when you get on a real bull they are a subconscious reaction. That's the only way it can happen. If you have to stop and think about it on the bull, it'll already be too late.... When I first started, I built a barrel and I practiced and practiced and within a year I was making my living riding bulls. I think I learned more on the barrel than I ever did on the bulls...."

Toward the end of the day, Mahan's students started sneaking looks at their watches and showing less eagerness when they called for another horse or bull to ride. Already the insides of most of their thighs were skinned down to raw patches of flesh. A twisted ankle or a sprained wrist had been enough to sideline the less enthusiastic students. Kids who had done farm work all their lives discovered their first real blisters where a bareback rigging had bound too hard or the wrap on a bull rope had taken a bite. They'd all been bruised. A few had bled. One kid had broken a tooth. Everyone looked hollow-eyed and beat, and they were all hurting. Mahan had cut them down to the point at which he figures they could probably start to learn.

Leffew, too, pushes his students to that point. "It's kind of like the marines," he says characteristically. "You've got to break them down to show them that what they're doing is wrong. I run in all my rank stock and make sure they get on something that throws them off. About the third day, they're sore and we take some time out and I start lecturing. I talk about positive thinking and my past experiences, about how I was nobody and couldn't ride anything. I tell them about the amazing transformations of positive thinking and how it helped me. I get the kids pumped up. I tell them a lot of stories about me and Donnie Gay, how in the mornings the first thing we'd do was to jump up and say: 'Goddam, I feel good!' Just to get the day started right. 'It's going to be a good day,' we'd say. 'We're going to win lots of money!' Then I match them against bulls I know they're going to ride. And by the end of the week, they're really riding good and they're really pumped up. I tell them that once they leave their schooling will really start. Whether they choose to go through the twenty-one-day image change is up to them; but it gives them a way to go when they leave...."

When Mahan finally called it a day in the arena a bunch of dirty, weary young cowboys wanted to limp off to the shower, eat dinner, and hit the sack. But school wasn't over yet.

"Men," Mahan announced, "after dinner I want everyone to stay in the dining room. We're going to go over the tapes we shot today. Then—if there's time—I want to show a couple of films."

The tough hands were up for it. They crowded the TV screen to watch the video playback. They asked questions and then hung on Mahan's answers. It seemed his message was getting through. One determined bareback rider had his

glove on during most of the viewing of the tapes. The squeak of each painful thrust of the rosined palm into the handle of his rigging cut through the cooling Texas night air.

The school would go on for two more days. A couple of students, tired as they were, would wait until the others were sleeping and then slip off in the night. This would end their short careers as rodeo cowboys, or at least it would until they could find a less rigorous means of pursuing them. The others would force their bruised bodies out of bed for a cup of coffee and breakfast before limping off to the arena. Mahan, not a man to show any unnecessary pity, would have them all run a couple of laps around the arena and then do some vigorous warm-up exercises down in the dirt in front of the chutes. After which it would all begin again. And by the afternoon of the third day, only the most committed, the ones that would finally find themselves going down the road on the pro circuit, would still be calling for that one more horse, that one more bull.

Beyond Little Britches and rodeo schools cowboys continue learning through imitation. Most good cowboys will admit to having had heroes. Monty Henson's hero was the great Casey Tibbs. To Gary Leffew, "George Paul was the greatest. He was my real hero. He kind of carried an aura with him; you just had to look at him. If I was at a rodeo and George was riding, I wouldn't let them go with me before he went. I would watch George ride and I was in awe—because he was always in control. He had so much energy flowing out of him that when he rode you almost felt sorry for the bull, no matter how rank he was, because George was the dominant factor. Instead of just hanging on and hoping he'd make it, George was in control all the time. It was like the bull was trying to get out from under him. He seemed to have the dominant mash on them. When I would watch George ride, the adrenalin would start running through me and my bull would suddenly look much smaller. I never got thrown off whenever George would ride before me. The year I won the championship was the year he got killed in his plane. And everytime I was up from then on I'd try and conjure up a vision of how George would handle my bull. And it was almost like George was riding the bull. I would feel like him sometimes. I would find myself making his moves."

31

GOIN' DOWN

THE ROAD

He's rosined his riggings
And laid back his wages.
He's dead set on riding
In the big rodeo.
                    —Billy Joe Shafer

The time it takes to ride a
bareback bronc or a bull is eight
seconds, and at the stock contrac-
tor's discretion saddle bronc riding
may be extended to ten seconds—
though this rarely happens. From
the grandstands, rodeo probably

looks like nice work. And even though, to the cowboy being whipped and battered and jerked about on the bucking animal, those eight or ten seconds might seem to stretch out to something like a lifetime, he'll usually admit that it's not so long. Not long or tough in terms of the time he spent and the problems he encountered just getting to the rodeo; in that respect there has been little change in cowboy life since the grueling days of riding trail on a herd up from Texas. Except that maybe now, it's a whole lot worse. Modern chain motels and fast-food shops across America are not much change from a bedroll in the middle of some new nowhere each night and the same monotonous campfire grub at mealtime. Those are still the basics, and barely that. And it's just as lonely out there as it ever was.

But to the cowboy, goin' down the road is a magical phrase. He complains about it constantly but he can't hide the hint of something in his voice that says he loves it as much as he hates it and that he hates going a lot less than he hates staying. Wrapped up in those four words—goin' down the road—is the very essence of who he is—and why: his history and heritage.

In order to live, a rodeo cowboy has to win. That's the name of the rodeo game. And in order to win, a cowboy needs to enter enough rodeos, get there, get on, and ride well enough on a good animal to score enough points to beat everyone else. Which is exactly the same idea most of the best men at each rodeo have.

At one point or another—usually in the beginning—the pressure of not having enough money hits almost every full-time rodeo hand. There are no salaries in this sport. And to further compound the financial problem, the cowboy is required to pay an entry fee to ride in a rodeo. These fees can be as high as one hundred dollars but the average is about thirty dollars per event per rodeo. Even the best cowboys have gone through hard times. Larry Mahan, who has probably won more money than any other man in the history of rodeo, thinks that for most cowboys financial problems never stop. "I would say that ninety percent of the cowboys goin' down the road today don't have enough money to go ahead and rodeo as they would like to. I had a family to think about. So I tried to work at all the rodeos, finding something on the labor list, running the catch pens or whatever position I could pick up. When you're bouncing around from one rodeo to the next and you're a good worker, the word gets out and it really isn't that tough. Of course it only pays like five dollars a performance, but if you go to seven or eight or ten performances a week—well, this is the gas from one rodeo to the next."

Cowboys winning money also seem to be lending money, helping a friend who isn't winning, chipping in for his entry fees, lending him a clean shirt, some jeans. There are guys out there who don't own one thing they're wearing; it's all on long-term loan from friends who know that tomorrow the tables could just as easily be turned.

Money is only one kind of

pressure that comes with goin' down the road. The actual travel is the worst part. It's hard, constant, relentless.

"We drive probably 150,000 miles a year," says Kaycee, Wyoming, bronc rider John "Witch" Holman. "A year ago I worked nine rodeos in five days and never slept in a bed. You'll spend twelve hours out of every twenty-four in a car, and driving just as hard as you can. And when you're not in a car, you're in a plane or something, or on a bus." Witch isn't really complaining. In the back of his voice is a kind of pride, a hint of the thrill and excitement which makes it impossible for him to contain a little smile of satisfaction.

Witch's friend and sometime traveling partner Chris LeDoux, a top-notch bareback bronc rider and singer with a number of albums to his credit, put it another way in the following song:

Faded old blue Wranglers
Dusty cowboy hat
Pair of scuffed-up boots upon
your feet
Can of pork and beans
That you open with your knife
It ain't much but it's all you've got
to eat.
You think of what your daddy
said:
If your money should run low
Just call— I'll send your bus fare
To come home.
But you're just too proud to take it
And home won't be the same
Now you've had a taste of Rodeo.
Chorus:
You set out on the road
To seek your boyhood dream,
To satisfy the hunger in your soul.
You wouldn't turn back now—
even if you could.
You were born to follow Rodeo.

All your money's gone
Except a twenty-dollar bill
But that's your fees to enter old
Cheyenne.
And all that's in your favor is
youth and your try
And a deep, gnawing, desperate
need to win.
As you step out on the highway
With your thumb up in the air
In your mind a promise has been
made:
If this way of life don't kill you
And you don't starve to death,
You swear you'll be the cham-
pion someday.
(Chorus)

In order to make it all work, the cowboy becomes his own travel agent. The telephone is his tool. He enters a rodeo a few days before it starts, with a promise to pay his fees—which he is required to do whether he shows up or not. The officials determine what and when a cowboy is to ride by drawing the cowboy's name and the number of an animal from a hat. The cowboy checks back to see what he has drawn. Being a gambler, he may have entered two rodeos for the same day, knowing that he will have to forfeit one entry fee. Some rodeos make it easier for the cowboy by allowing him to trade days and positions with other cowboys so he can adjust his schedule. But most rodeos don't; the cowboy is expected to pay his fees and show up on a certain day. So a cowboy serious about winning will be constantly working days in advance to try to determine where he can go to be mounted best and win the most. Being a good rider is only one part of rodeo. Knowing how to travel is almost as important. The ability to work out the best itinerary can often make the difference between a winner and a loser.

"You choose this life, or it chooses you," says one seasoned hand. "It sounds strange, but once you're in it there's not much you can do about it. So you learn to live with it." Living with it involves a near-starvation diet in times of low funds, an appetite for hardship, and a penchant for gambling. Some cowboys are content to win just enough to keep goin' down the road. A lot of others want to win world championships, which involves a great deal more than just learning to live with rodeo life. Cowboys estimate—conservatively—that the minimum number of rodeos a man must compete in to have even a fair chance at winning a world title is one hundred per year. Larry Mahan, Bobby Berger, Gary Leffew, Joe Alexander, Jerome Robinson, and John MacBeth all average far more than that. Don Gay, the 1974 World Champion Bull Rider, mounted bulls at 160 rodeos. These were all in different cities and towns, requiring him to travel as far as two thousand miles after climbing off a bull one night in order to be able to get onto another one the next afternoon.

According to Monty Henson, the 1975 Saddle Bronc Champion, "The Fourth of July all the way through the month of August is the hardest part about rodeoing. The nine days around the Fourth, which they call the cowboy's Christmas, are the worst. I started my run last year on the twenty-seventh of June in Yukon, Oklahoma. The next day I drove over to Casville, Missouri. The next day I was in Ponca, Nebraska. The thirtieth I was in Greeley, Colorado. The first I went up to Williams Lake, Alberta, Canada, and Ponoka, Alberta—worked both of them in one day. The sec-

ond I was in Montalto, Alberta, and went on to Calgary for the third. We left Calgary right after the rodeo on the afternoon of the third, nine of us in a van—we had to leave our clothes because there wasn't enough room, just took rigging bags—and drove down to work the gateways: Cody, Wyoming; Red Lodge, Montana; and Livingston, Montana. They all go on the fourth. We drove all night long, got up and went to all three rodeos that day. That night, after Livingston was over, we drove to Billings. Got there about two in the morning. I had to fly out that morning for Phoenix, so I could get on a bronc in Prescott, Arizona. The cowboy's Christmas! I'll tell you what, those few days right there nearly killed me."

It's a fast life. Schedules are tight and little things like an airplane landing fifteen minutes late can cause problems. "Even if a guy drives a hundred miles an hour," Witch Holman confesses, "he sometimes won't make it. Once we

were working Yuma and another little town down in Colorado. We got in late and were driving pretty fast to get to Yuma. Just as we pulled into town the police started after us. We wouldn't stop. We just kept going. Finally, they ran us off the road to get us stopped and asked what the deal was. We told them and— hell—they just got in front of us and took us down to the rodeo. Ivan Daines just barely had time to get on his bronc. I'll tell you what, it's a rat race."

Ironically, the better the cowboy gets in terms of ability and winning, the harder the travel is.

Some successful cowboys have earned enough in rodeo to afford to buy and operate their own airplanes, thereby cutting out the necessity of keeping to some almost impossible airlines schedules or trying to charter planes and pilots to take them where and when they want to go. Larry Mahan looks at it as a curse and a blessing. "Because I know I can go," he says, "I will go. And sometimes I push myself harder than I should, entering more rodeos, spending more hours in the air, losing sleep, tearing down the old body." Johnny Quintana, the 1972 World Champion Bull Rider, agrees: "I put a little better than four hundred hours on my airplane in three months this summer—that's almost living in it. It's pretty hard when you're working five or six rodeos a week. It just wears you out and you find yourself sleeping standing up."

Bobby Berger has put thousands of rodeo miles on his little plane. His will to get to a rodeo is so unswerving it amounts to obsession. He'll do almost anything to show up to mount out a really good bronc. Recently, he was flying his plane into Douglas, Wyoming, for the State Fair rodeo. He knew he'd be running a tight photo-finish to make it in time for the bronc riding. He had estimated his fuel at enough to reach the Douglas airport with at least twenty-five miles to spare. Everything looked good. He'd just have time to cinch up, measure off his rein, and fork himself down into the saddle. Then he discovered one of the seals had given out on a fuel tank and gas was leaking back over the wing. He was fifty miles from Douglas. The engine gave its first cough. Out of gas. Bobby bellied the little plane down for a bounce-and-spark landing on the freeway. He left the plane there, flagged down the first car and got the driver to take him to the arena. He was just being driven up behind the chutes when he heard the announcer say they had turned out his bronc. Which, he shrugged, is the way it goes.

A bull rider or a bronc rider might be free to fly to all his rodeos. But a man in the roping and steer-wrestling events needs to haul a horse with him. Ernie Taylor remembers how it was in 1973 when he was out chasing the big gold and silver World Champion Calf Roper buckle: "Every time I'd stop to fill up with gas, the attendant would have to wake me up to get me to pay. I'd have my head on the steering wheel, trying to get a little bit of rest. I could have gone to sleep at the wheel and killed myself. But rodeo's that kind of sport. It's what you have to do. I don't know any other professional athlete or any other businessman who really does that sort of thing to make his living."

Two recent developments put a near-tragic cramp in the style of the rodeo cowboy: the price of gasoline and the fifty-five-mile-an-hour speed limit. Being natural hustlers, the cowboys found a way around the energy crisis. They found they could squeeze one more man into an already overcrowded car to help with the increased cost of things; then, taking a lesson from the truck drivers, they installed citizen-band radios in many of their rigs and found they could avoid the economic hazards of speed traps. "It doesn't take away all the danger of running into Old Smokey (Smokey the Bear, as the highway patrolmen are fondly called)," a roper laughed. "But it sure as hell cuts it down to something a cowboy can handle."

I've seen it work. Last summer, afraid I wouldn't make it across two states to a rodeo the next day, a cowboy said: "Follow me." He had a pickup and a long horse trailer. We drove at eighty miles an hour for four hundred seventy-five miles with only two slowdowns—one for a speed trap he had been warned about by truckers, and another when we sighted an oncoming patrol car.

Naturally, the cowboy would have a C.B. radio. He is a man of the times. He always was. It is merely the nature of his work and the romantic mold into which he has been cast that give him the air of being some kind of historical holdover. The truth is, he is a jet-age man in a jet-age business. And his only real cover is the big hat, the high-heeled boots, and a cool devil-be-damned attitude.

In a lot of ways, the traditional image of the cowboy doesn't serve the rodeo cowboy well. That tall, warped, old cowpoke taking an easy moment to lean against a corral post and roll his own smoke is about as far as you can get from the professional rodeo cowboy. These men are athletes of the highest order. They're concerned about the condition of their bodies as much as any athlete. A number of them are food fadists and vitamin fanatics. They exercise—on the road, in cars, in motel pools and rooms, in spas and gyms—wherever they can, trying to keep their bodies toned up to take

the battering they receive rodeo after rodeo, day in and day out. Part of the try, the confidence, the whole mental thing they have about riding an animal and winning comes through the assurance that they are in good physical shape. Isometrics and those little exercising devices small enough to fit in a jacket pocket make it possible for a cowboy to work out in motel rooms and the back seats of moving cars.

The secret to making ends meet and staying on the road is being able to keep going, to stay in competition. Rodeo is a dangerous sport. There are few fatalities, but there is a serious injury to some cowboy at, on the average, every other rodeo. And although the cowboys are insured through the PRCA, the coverage is barely sufficient to help them avoid the embarrassment of having to dodge a huge hospital bill.

Cowboys are obsessed with their sport. Injuries don't seem to make them want to quit. They can't wait to get back in action. It is inevitable that at any rodeo there will be one or more cowboys riding or roping or steer wrestling while still wearing a cast. And if the cast gets in the way of what they want to do, they'll cut away the part that's causing the problem or just take off the whole thing. There are numerous stories of cowboys who have spent much of the night before a rodeo soaking a cast off a broken leg in a bathtub so they could get on a bronc the next day.

Dennis Reiners is a perfect case in point. Ringtail, as he is known, has broken his legs so many times he knows exactly what kind of cast he needs and how long he will need to wear it. Recently, in fact, he designed his own earth-boot cast. He took a new pair of cowboy boots and worked over the boot for his broken leg with a knife and a punch, cutting out the toe and making the boot so it would lace up the front. He attached a stiff nylon brace as a splint and then poured liquid foam inside and let that set up and form to his leg. He had a shoemaker lower the heels on both boots and add an extra thickness of leather to raise the soles. Then, a couple of days after breaking his leg and working on the boot-cast, he was back in the arena—with a striped vest and a clipboard, acting as a cowboy judge.

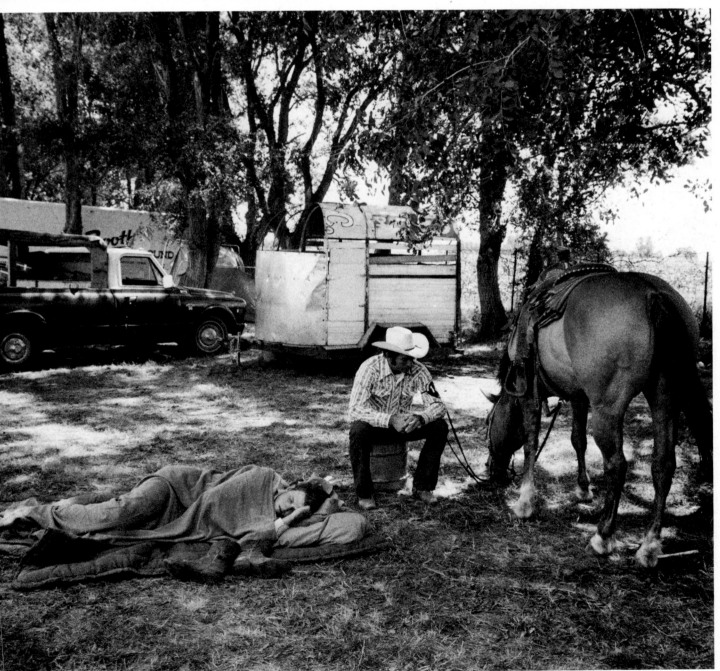

BEHIND T

E CHUTES

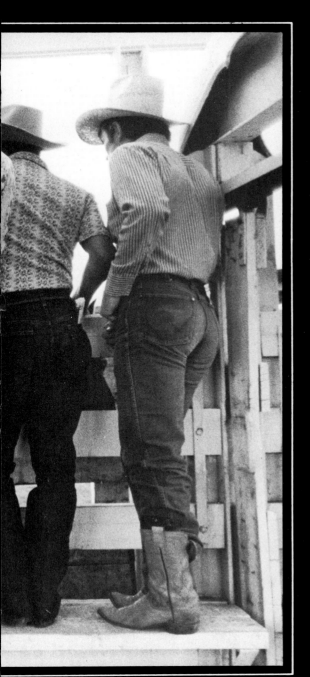

No one can seriously try to understand the complexities of rodeo and the cowboy life without at least one glimpse behind the chutes. There, in the dirt and weeds and the old discarded Lily cups of small-town arenas or the cold concrete walkways of big-city coliseums, it is almost possible to see the whole rodeo ridden before it even begins.

Cowboys start showing up

about an hour early, dragging in their canvas duck rigging bags, stowing them in a corner, against a fence. A cowboy keeps his riggings and ropes, chaps and spurs, and all the other odds and ends of his rodeo gear in his bag. Sometimes, when the pace is fast and traveling space is limited, a rigging bag will have to double as makeshift suitcase and catchall. Understandably, a rigging bag can reflect a great deal of a cowboy's personality and interests. Some of them are so tidy they seem almost to crackle when they are opened; others just ooze their assorted contents, which can include—aside from the basic cowboy tools—anything from last week's dirty shorts to love letters and melted chocolate bars.

One thing that has always fascinated me about the scene behind the chutes is the ritual of the taping of limbs. It's like a field hospital back there. The strident sound of adhesive tape being ripped off the roll is constant—feet, yards, even miles of sticky white tape. Cowboys tape their fingers, toes, ankles, wrists, thighs, ribs. And if they aren't using tape, they're binding their bodies with big Ace bandages, tying wide elastic layers around the muscles and joints, even wrapping them on the outside of their jeans, crisscrossing the wraps to let a kneecap or the point of an elbow show through. There are also a few of those weird surgical appliances: bright stainless-steel bracing with neat little precision joints all fitted out with discs and screws and bits of covered foam, the tight cotton sleeves closing with laces and a row of buckles.

As in a lot of athletic situations, much of the binding and taping is probably legitimate as an essential reinforcement of a previously injured area. But often it appears—especially in the younger cowboys—to be simply some necessary psychological aid, a kind of temporary bandaging to help the cowboy get himself together and over the chute gate for his ride.

Most cowboys don't contest in their regular street boots—if they even bother wearing cowboy boots outside of the arena. In their rigging bags they keep a pair of riding boots—all scuffed and patched and stitched, evidence of the rough treatment a man's feet and legs get inside the chutes. Riding boots are usually no different from street boots, which they probably once were; they've just done more miles. Occasionally, too, a cowboy will have done some makeshift modifications on either the tops or vamps or both with a pocketknife or a leather punch. If you ask a cowboy why he prefers to ride in boots with age-softened tops and worn-out soles he'll probably tell you that worn-in boots give him the feeling of the stirrups and they register the stroke of the spurs.

Bareback riders, whose event generally starts the rodeo program, crack out their equipment first, taking time to check their riggings and prepare their gloves. Saddle-bronc riders sit in their saddles, testing the length of their stirrup leathers, making sure all the rivets and bindings are sound. And bull riders will probably tie their plaited ropes to a railing or a fence post and begin cleaning it carefully with a pocket-knife and a wire brush.

A good man is particular about his equipment. He will usually do anything he can to help another cowboy; but he hates to let someone use his gear. Which might seem strange considering that it is all built according to a pretty explicit set of standards outlined and approved by the Professional Rodeo Cowboys Association. In most cases, it has been designed with two things in mind: to force the cowboy to work to display his skills, and to allow the animal almost all the advantages. But just because a rigging or a saddle or a rope is standard doesn't mean it's going to be the same. There are little things, almost hidden sometimes, that make one saddle far superior to others, that make one rigging ride easier, that make one bull rope better to pull and wrap. Whatever it is, to the cowboy it's significant. Either the maker did it through intention or accident or the cowboy gradually got it worked down to the point of being special—whether in actual fact or in his mind.

A cowboy's gear can **assume an importance above everything else in his life, including his wife and family.** (Which may be one of a number of reasons rodeo marriages are often doomed.) This preoccupation with equipment is hardly unfounded. As Larry Mahan pointed out to his students, the best you can get is barely good enough. It can make the difference between winning and losing, the difference between life and death.

A cowboy can't afford not to go over his equipment before every rodeo. Heat, damp, dry, cold—all have noticeable effects on hemp and leather, requiring him to make adjustments and changes. Still, the amount of time a cowboy gives to this ritual checking seems excessive. It does until you realize that it really has little to do with the equipment. The procedure lets him look beyond the rigging or the glove, to get into himself, and to start getting up for the ride he is going to make.

Behind the chutes, winning is the main word in a cowboy's mind. Each one sees it in a different way, just as each reaches his particular high in a different way. One man might get pumped up knowing his horse will fight in the chute or that the bull he's drawn will come out hooking and hunting the man before he's even on the ground.

By now, what Gary Leffew brought to rodeo with his own reading of Maxwell Maltz's Psycho-Cybernetics, and his attempts at putting it into practice behind the chutes and in the arena, are legendary. "I got into reading these positive-thinking books while I was laying around one winter after I hadn't been winning much. And I started seeing what I had been doing to myself. I was defeating my purpose. I was actually hypnotizing myself into believing that I couldn't win. So I changed my whole self-image and set my goal for the world's championship. That first year, I ended up second. The next year I ended up third, but I won more money than I did the previous year. And then the third year I did win the world's championship.

What I did was go through a twenty-one-day self-image change—the same thing I teach now in my bull-riding schools. The reason you use twenty-one days is that it takes twenty-one days for anything to become a habit. You are a victim of your self-image, which is made up of all your past experiences; you have this blueprint in your self-conscious mind of who you are and what you can do. The magic thing is that while you are a victim of it you can change your self-image, re-record it. You can record in there whatever you want to be. I wanted to become the World's Champion Bull Rider. So I reprogrammed myself to get the habit of success. And at the end of that twenty-one days, where I had been six months without riding a bull before, I felt I could ride a red-eyed lion. I had inner confidence I'd never felt before. I didn't hope I was going to be a success, I knew I was."

What the books Leffew had discovered said about positive thinking was not exactly new to the rodeo cowboy. But, partly out of embarrassment and partly out of that sheer Western refusal to display the kind of self-consciousness they associated with Eastern people, nobody in rodeo had ever put it into words. Not clear, succinct words that made psyching up for a ride sound almost scientific. Before long, Leffew had a lot of cowboys reading the books. They read them and nodded their heads and said:

Yeah, that's what I've been doing all along.

Behind the chutes, the positive mental attitude is as strong as ozone. And it increases with the size and seriousness of the rodeo. A little punkin roller out in Nebraska or up in Oregon is certain to have its share of confused kids, weekend saddle tramps out to impress a girlfriend, and maybe an old has-been with a fifth of Jim Beam washing under his belt for courage—cowboys with nothing more on their minds than the vague thought that it sure would be nice to go the full eight seconds. But the pro, the cowboy who's chasing one of those big trophy buckles and trying to make a living at rodeo, doesn't look at it that way at all. He's going to win. Behind the chutes at Cheyenne or Houston or the National Finals Rodeo in Oklahoma City, where the stakes are high and every cowboy is bent on winning, the air is charged with intense, deadly seriousness.

Unlike most professional sports, there are no rules to regulate a cowboy's training, no contract stipulating when he is to get to a rodeo, and no pressure on him to do well or even to do it at all. Once he has met the simple rules of entering a rodeo, the cowboy answers to no one except himself. And for that reason, most of the best cowboys goin' down the road are tough taskmasters.

Traveling with Larry Mahan when he's in a storm and riding badly is an unforgettable experience. I was on a run with him one summer when he repeatedly messed up good broncs and bucked off his bulls at rodeos in Salt Lake City, Ogden, and Cheyenne. He retreated into a silence that grew increasingly

deeper and darker as the days wore on. He entered rodeos as though they were a punishment and forced himself to make them all. He doubled his workout schedule and clamped down on his diet. He didn't let up until he proved to himself that he could still win.

Getting psyched up for a **ride is a different process for every cowboy. They all agree that it has to happen. But each man finds his own level.** Gary Leffew feels "the real secret is defeating the bull before you ever get on him. You have to defeat him in your own mind. You have to see yourself riding him and jumping off and the crowd cheering." What and how much Leffew sees is important to the success of his ride. "I form a mental picture of myself on the bull, just sitting up there, riding him, spurring him, and looking pretty. The more vivid you can make the picture, the better results you get from it. It's really a good feeling when you ride a real rank one and jump off and raise your hands and the crowd goes wild. I think that's one of the things that keeps me in rodeo, because I have a need for that."

The only picture a champion can have is positive. "If you go in there thinking <u>I can't ride this bull</u>," says Phil Lyne, "he's already got you bucked off." He feels this applies to the timed events as well. "In the roping, if you back into the box and lack confidence in your horse or think you've got a calf

there's no way you can place on, you're just not mentally ready to win anything. You're already beat before you nod your head."

Leffew points out that "one of the worst things a guy can do is think about what the bull is going to do to you. Someone will tell you, 'Boy, this bull turns back. He's strong. He'll hook you.' They tell you all the bad things and you worry about them. But the thing these positive-thinking books have taught me is to worry constructively. Worry about all the good things that are going to happen. This bull's going to turn back and really buck. By his doing that you're really going to score high."

The cowboy gets the winning picture established in his mind according to how his own personality can handle it. Some cowboys become outwardly aggressive— talking, moving, pumping up and down on the front of a chute gate, doing exercises that make their chaps fly and their spurs ring. Both Jerome Robinson and Don Gay build themselves up to such an intensity that their faces go white. Steve Cosca, bareback bronc and bull rider stomps around and snorts like a bull. Larry Mahan says: "I just walk up and down and tell myself that I'm an animal. I get worked up to the point where I'm so aggressive that there's no way I'm going to blow it. I refuse to let a negative thought come into my mind."

Cosca tries to put himself in a vacuum. "I try to forget about everybody. I block everbody out of my mind and go over what I'm going to do. I walk and keep warmed up: kneebends, pull-ups, touch my toes. And while I'm doing this I'm going over in my mind the ride I'm going to make. I see my glove tied on my hand, how my rigging's set, where I'm going to have my feet on the chute gate. When I nod my head, I see how the gate's going to open, see myself reaching and spurring the horse out. Good, solid, hard strokes. Trying to get my feet into him. I try to work this all out in my mind while I'm walking around. Then I'll stop and sit down and just calmly think about it. Then, remembering any mistakes I've made on a horse in the past, I put them in a little black box in my mind and pretend I'm flying along in an airplane and just drop the box with all these bad habits out so I'll never see it again."

Other riders turn the entire process inward. They hardly move at all, becoming silent, steely, insulating themselves, brooding, brooding. This kind of cowboy ignores everything except the ride that is going on in his mind. Joe Alexander and Bill Smith get this way—

quiet, thoughtful, remote. Their championship records show that it's right for them: Alexander has been World Champion Bareback Rider four years in a row; Smith has been World Champion Saddle Bronc Rider three different years. There can be definite results from the images screened inside all that silence.

Fortunately, Larry Mahan, who is constantly set upon by the press, doesn't need silence. In fact, he thrives on noise, confusion, and the constant challenge of keeping two or three things going at one time. However, no matter how much is happening outside, he doesn't lose sight of his single most important goal. "When I'm really up for a ride," he admits, "and I know it's going to be a tough ride, that there's a lot at stake, I'm to the point where I can still think about it and communicate with the outside world. I can sit and talk to the press,

to a TV interviewer, or even just somebody in the audience; but still—in the back of my mind—I'm making my ride over and over and over."

One thing behind the chutes is the same for every man. He wants to know as much as he can about the animal he has drawn. Certain animals—V61, Oscar, Midnight— become as notorious as the best cowboys. They go a season without being ridden and their fame grows and spreads. Cowboys watch them, analyze their bucking patterns, and try to figure out the moves it will take to make an eight-second ride. No matter how a cowboy channels this information into his mind, if he does it positively it will make his ride better. Even if a cowboy has ridden the animal before, he'll still ask everyone else about him. He wants to compare what they tell him with what he already knows; he wants to be familiar with all the possibilities, all the variations, how the horse or bull bucks in different situations and conditions. The better the animal is, the ranker he is, the more the cowboy wants to know. Have you had him? they ask. Have you seen him buck? What does he do? How is he in the chute? Does he turn back? How much rein do I need? Is he fast? Does he spin? To the best cowboy this information is all positive reinforcement. He feeds it into his mind—many of them liken it to computer input—and gradually comes up with the picture of the ride he's got to make, complete with a strategy pattern that includes every possible mood and move a horse or bull could have or make. The result is as clear and crisp as a strip of well-shot film, framed and focused as fully as the cowboy needs to have it in order to see himself riding his animal from start to finish, from the chute to the whistle and safely on the ground. Winning.

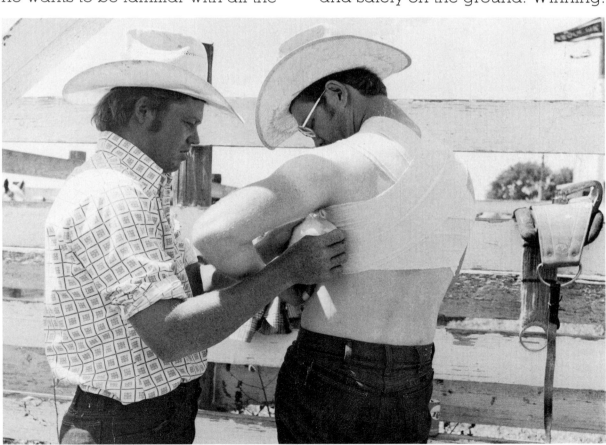

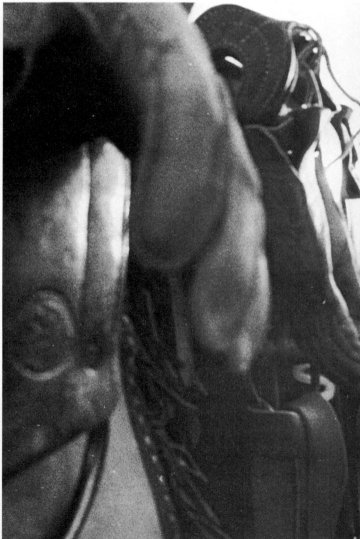

54

ANIMALS AND THE LUCK O'

THE DRAW

The real impact of good rodeo depends, finally, on the animals. It is a rugged, violent sport, and in order to keep it this way there must always be animals of the highest quality, animals with enough strength and heart to create a challenge for cowboys whose total mental and physical powers have been pumped up and brought to bear on making a winning ride. Rodeo can congratulate itself that it hasn't fallen into what Ernest Hemingway felt was the shame of modern bullfighting, that the bulls were gradually all being bred down to accomodate stylish though mediocre matadors. The exact opposite is happening in rodeo. Stock contractors are constantly trying to breed and buy better bulls and bucking horses, stronger dogging steers, and stouter, faster-running calves.

About twenty-one stock contractors supply the animals to more than 600 professional rodeos in America. Because their reputations and the number of significant contracts they can get are based on the quality of their bucking stock, these companies are always on the lookout for new and better animals. Good broncs and bulls are hard to come by, so they are pampered and protected. Ordinarily, rodeo animals are in the arena fewer than five minutes a year. They are transported to and from rodeos as carefully as any supervaluable cargo and fed like reigning royalty.

The cowboys welcome better stock. Their success, the success of their talents and their ability to win, depends on the animal. "If you've drawn an animal that makes an average, half-hearted attempt at bucking you off," Larry Mahan declares, "an animal that just comes out and bloop-bloops along, you might make your eight seconds and spur

up a storm, but you're not going to win any money."

A cowboy wants to get animals with heart, with as much beardown and try as he's got himself. Cowboys call it the luck of the draw. A few days before the rodeo begins the officials determine who will ride what on which day by drawing names and numbers from a hat. By their very nature and spirit, the best cowboys are born gamblers; they will often enter two or three rodeos on the same day and then wait until after the stock is drawn to see where they can go to get on the toughest animal. Generally, that is the only variable they consider. If the difference between two rodeos is traveling 50 miles or 1500 miles and the better animal is at the 1500-mile rodeo, it is inevitable that the cowboy will drive or fly the extra 1450 miles to get on it.

JUDGES

The cowboy judges—the
men in the arena who determine
the points for each ride—must be
working cowboy members of the
PRCA, with enough years of experience to enable them to determine
the quality of a ride quickly and
accurately. This is no easy feat. The
action in rodeo is fast, and in order
to see it and be able to call it the
judge must put himself in a relative-
ly dangerous position. To further

compound matters, the judges are very often cowboys on the injured list, on crutches, in casts, or otherwise unable to compete.

Two men judge the riding events. Each judge scores the rider from 1 to 25 points and the animal from 1 to 25 points. They combine these scores to make a total of 100 points possible, 50 for the man, 50 for the animal.

The difficult thing in judging rodeo is not making the decision itself but how fast it must be made. The scores must be tallied and given to the announcer and rodeo secretary between the time the particular ride being judged ends and the next one begins, which can be as brief as a few seconds.

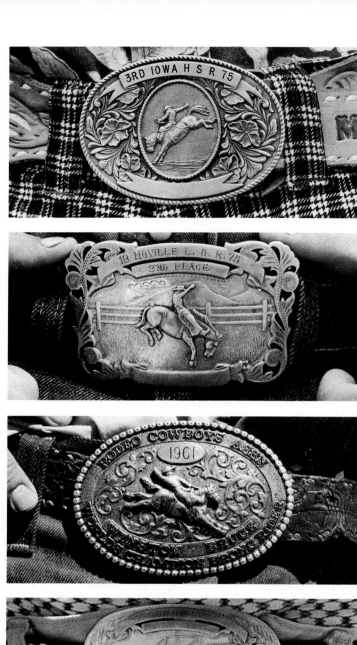

SADDLE BR

NC RIDING

The first image anyone has of rodeo—the standard image—is probably the right one. It's usually of a stout horse at the peak of a high, full-powered sunfish buck, with the rider glued up there, poised, his spurs stuck smartly into the front end, over the points of the shoulders and just starting to make a smooth raking stroke back to the cantle. It is also the symbol of the Professional

Rodeo Cowboys Association. They print it hard-edged, in black; we are most likely to see it in a sepia haze. That the PRCA should have chosen the image and we should see it as the symbol of rodeo makes sense. Rodeo probably did start with the saddle bronc, the horse nobody could break, the animal untamed and recalcitrant as the West, before anyone added the Spanish name, before any crowd gathered to watch.

As opposed to most of the rest of rodeo—except calf roping—saddle bronc riding is a classy event. It is a natural showcase for cowboy style and skill. It doesn't require as much actual brute strength as either the bareback bronc riding or bull riding. What it does take is a combination of precise coordination, a keen sense of balance, and a dancer's love of rhythm.

The saddle used by bronc riders—they call it the Association saddle—is built on a standard tree with the following specifications:

Fork: 14 inches wide
9 inches maximum height
5¾-inch gullet
Cantle: 5 inches maximum height
14 inches maximum width

Things were not always so explicit. There used to be saddles called freaks, which the cowboys had designed in such a way that there was almost no chance for a bronc to buck them off. One old-timer from Montana, Lyman Brewster, told me he once had a saddle so finely tailored to the fit of his body that he almost had to be put in it with a shoehorn. These old saddles had high-dished cantles (or seats) and forks with wide undercut swells—and those sometimes even beefed up with buck-rolls.

The advantages of the stan-

dard saddle are obvious. First, it promotes fair competition among the cowboys and is not simply a test of a saddlemaker's skill. Second, with the design of the present Association saddle, the horse is given an edge over the cowboy and makes him work for his win.

Bronc riders use a single rein made of rough four-plait braided manila rope. The rein is approximately six feet long and increases in thickness from the point where it attaches to the halter until it is about one and a half inches thick where the rider holds it. It is loosely braided, which allows it some stretch and give and also allows the cowboy's fingers to bite into it and not slip during the ride. The length and feel of the rein can make a great deal of difference to

a cowboy's being able to ride with perfect balance and timing.

There is something special about every piece of equipment in the rodeo business. Each event has its specific model of spurs. The spurs for saddle bronc riding have a short shank—one and a half inches—and they can either be straight or angled in slightly—from seven to fifteen degrees. They are fitted with a small dull rowel like a five-point star—dull so it won't cut the horse, star-shaped so it will roll.

A bronc rider's chaps are sturdier than those worn by men in the other events. The leather is thicker and they have stronger straps to bind them to the upper leg. The reason for this is that he needs more protection in the chute and then when he rides, he actually grips the saddle with his legs. In order to increase friction and hold the swells of the saddle the rider will usually apply dry powdered rosin to the area of his chaps that come in contact with the fork.

A saddle bronc rider doesn't bind on his boots as the bareback bronc riders and bull riders do. There is always the danger that he might buck off and get a foot hung up in a stirrup. If this happens—and it does—he wants his boots to slip off easily and release him. Some cowboys take a knife and slice the tops of their boots to lessen the danger of a hang-up. Most of them sprinkle the insides with talcum powder and wear slick nylon socks.

All the rodeo events have one thing in common: Every part of the preride preparation is important. This holds true especially in the saddle bronc riding. The balance and timing of a ride are affected by the way the saddle is adjusted to the cowboy and how it is set on the horse. A cowboy will work for hours adjusting his stirrup leathers and bind straps. Just as important is how he estimates and measures off the rein to find where he will take his hold. The average horse takes a rein that is a fist-and-thumb beyond the swell of the saddle when the rein is drawn straight back from the halter. If the cowboy knows that a horse bucks with his head down he will allow for this by riding a longer rein, and he'll take a shorter one for a horse that bucks with its head up.

Getting down and ready on a bronc is dangerous business. The chute can become a treacherous trap if the horse has a tendency to fight. The cowboy usually tries to calm his horse before he ever starts saddling up. He works close and keeps some contact with him. A man with a touchy horse will stay near him while he's waiting his turn. He'll be touching the horse on the neck, stroking it, keeping it quiet for the moment when he'll climb down into the saddle. Then, when his time comes, he'll try to ease into the saddle and get out into the arena as fast as possible. The thing a bronc rider fears most is being mounted, feet in the stirrups, and then having the horse blow up, rare over, and mash him back against the chute gate.

When the chute gate opens, the rider must have his feet up front, over the points of the horse's shoulders. This is called marking the horse out. His spurs must be there when the horse's front feet hit the ground on that first jump out of the chute. Then he finds the timing of the horse's bucking pattern and falls into it with his spurring. As the horse is kicking high with his hind feet, the rider's feet are crammed ahead, spurs over the points of the shoulders; then when the horse's hind feet are on the ground and he is jumping forward, the rider's spurs are raking back and up toward the cantle. In this way he sets up a rhythmical pattern that experienced bronc riders say is as simple and natural as rocking in a rocking chair. At the same time, a good rider keeps constant pressure on his rein, not pumping on it, but holding it out in front of his body and using it to help him maintain his poise and balance.

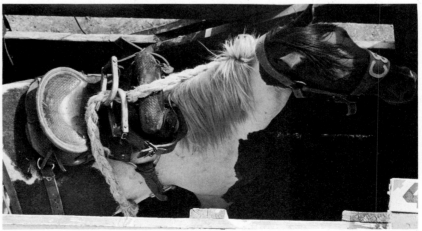

LF ROPING

There are two events in rodeo that probably require more skill than any of the other events—that's saddle bronc riding and calf roping. In both of these events there's more equipment and more things that can go wrong," states Canadian calf roper Jim Gladstone. And Ernie Taylor, who was the 1973 World Champion Calf Roper and who is not particularly modest about what he's done and what it means, says simply: "Calf roping is an art. The name of the game is speed. The fastest time always wins. The secret of success is getting your time and your moves down to perfection."

Calf roping is the one rodeo event still universally practiced on the ranch. In the arena, it's a race against time. Unlike the rough events out of the bucking chutes in which the scoring is done largely on quality and style, the calf roping winners are determined entirely by the stopwatch. The cowboys are out to beat the fastest time. It's that clear-cut. And one major pump-up for a roper is to watch the men going before him. They clock a certain time; he knows he's got to beat it. If someone ropes and ties a calf in 9.4 seconds, there is always the chance that the next man will win with a 9.3 time. It's uncanny how often it happens. Phil Lyne and Barry Burke are notorious for being able to somehow trim down the time by a tenth of a second. Phil, who was in 1971 and 1972 both World Champion Calf Roper and World Champion All-Around Cowboy, and who ranks with Larry Mahan and Jim Shoulders as one of the best cowboys in the history of rodeo, claims he thrives on this kind of pressure.

A calf roper's most valuable asset is the horse he rides. How much of the credit for consistent good run should go to the horse is difficult to say. Jim Gladstone feels a horse is at least seventy-five percent responsible for winning. Other ropers say sixty-five percent. Phil Lyne, noted for his ability to rope well anytime, anywhere, off of a number of borrowed horses, cuts it down to fifty percent. Whatever amount of credit the horse deserves, to be good in the arena it must have two basic qualities—a capability for a sudden, sustained burst of speed and a calm disposition. Because both of these qualities are common to the quarter horse, it is the animal most ropers choose to ride. They all know exactly what they want in a horse. "I like a horse that is good in the box," Jim Gladstone says. "I want him to stand perfectly still until I give the calf a head start. Then I want him to start and run straight, to go right up behind the calf, and to stop straight when I catch him."

This sounds easier than it is. And a horse that can do it, a horse that consistently puts a man in the prize money is hard to come by. Dean Oliver, eight-time winner of the World Champion Calf Roper title, feels "all horses are individuals, they all have different personalities just like people. Every one of them is different. That's why a good one is hard to find. And that's why a good one is worth a lot of money."

The ropes cowboys use are tightly twisted grass (manila) or poly fiber 3/8th to 7/16th of an inch thick and between twenty-five and thirty feet long. They choose their fiber, weight, and length according to what feels most comfortable to them. The manila ropes are said to have the most life, but they require more care, break more readily, and are more responsive to weather

conditions. In addition to his lariat—he may carry two—a roper has a shorter, smaller, length of rope called a pigging string, which he uses to tie the calf's feet. He carries the loop end of the pigging string in his teeth until he has caught the calf. Usually, he will carry a spare pigging string tucked in his belt.

The calf is held in a narrow chute fitted with a set of spring-loaded doors. The roper rides his horse back into a deep three-sided chute the cowboys call the box. The front of the chute is then closed off with a taut piece of rope called the barrier. When the roper signals he is ready, the calf is released. It has a ten-to-fifteen-foot start, depending on the length of the arena, then the barrier snaps open and the roper is free to pursue the calf (if the horse runs through the barrier before the calf has its proper head start, the roper is automatically fined ten seconds). The roper catches the calf, throws him down, and ties any three feet. The tie must hold for six seconds.

Calf ropers lead a different rodeo life than bronc riders and bull riders. Rarely do they travel as hard and as far. Their mobility is limited by the fact that they need to pull a trailer for their horses. Occasionally, a roper going hard for the championship will fly part of the time and drive part of the time, using his own horse when he can, borrowing someone else's the rest of the time.

BARE-BACK BACK BRO

NC RIDING

The only solid tie bareback bronc riding has to the rest of rodeo tradition is that it pits a man against a horse. It is a tremendous challenge for the man. The horses in this event tend to be smaller and faster than saddle broncs, and they have a snakier bucking style. Bareback bronc riding is wild and showy, characterized by aggressive, exaggerated spurring. Most cowboys will say that physically it is the most demanding event in the sport. "It's harder on your body," says Rusty Riddle, a first-rate bareback bronc rider from Mineral Wells, Texas, "it takes more try than any other event, and it's harder to get up for."

Bareback bronc riders are the most obsessive about their equipment. They seem to spend more time with their rigging, both working at it and making certain it doesn't get abused during travel. The rigging is made of leather that is sometimes laminated with rawhide for body and stiffness. It measures about twenty-two inches in length, ten inches wide at the center where the handhold is fixed, and tapers to six inches at the ends, where metal D-rings attach it to the latigoes and cinch. A single handhold of rawhide and leather is attached to the center of the rigging. It is generally crafted to fit a specific rider's hand. He wants it snug and comfortable and will spend hours with a knife, sandpaper, and rosin working and molding the handhold until it conforms to the grip of his palm.

The second vital piece of bareback gear is the glove. It is no ordinary glove, and some cowboys treat them as if they were fetishes. They are specially made of goatskin or steerhide. The cowboy tailors it down to his hand. He trims out excess bits of leather from the seams and re-sews various parts. Sometimes he cuts the ends off a couple of fingers, or all of them, or one finger and the thumb. He applies rosin to the palm. The first time, he burns the rosin in so it penetrates and forms a base which stiffens the palm. He powders on more rosin and works it down to the consistency he feels is right. Once he has it right, he protects the glove as best he can, keeping it where it will stay clean and not be crushed.

The spurs worn by bareback bronc riders differ from the saddle bronc rider's in that they have a slightly longer shank—two inches—and are either straight or only slightly angled in—five degrees. The rowels are a little larger than saddle bronc rowels. And they spin free, like wheels to help the cowboy's spurring action.

Under no circumstances does the bareback bronc rider want his boots to pull off during the ride. To keep this from happening, he fastens a strap about an inch and a half wide tightly around the tops of his boots.

Chaps are not necessary in this event. However, they do provide leg protection inside the chute, and by flapping and whipping with the snatch and jerk of the bucking and spurring, they make the ride look showier and might even cause the horse to buck better and harder.

The cowboy sets his rigging on the back slope of the horse's withers. He has a couple of other cowboys help him with the final cinching; they usually work from both sides so the tension is even and the rigging will stay sitting straight on the horse during the ride.

A few minutes before his time to go, the bareback rider climbs over the chute and gets down on his horse. He puts on his glove then, binding the top of it to his wrist by taking a couple of wraps with a narrow strap and then tying it off. When the horse before his goes out into the arena, he starts working his glove into the handhold. He pushes it in slowly, getting it right, finding that place where there is a perfect fit of hand and glove and rigging.

At the last moment, the rider scoots up close to the rigging, almost sitting on his hand in the handhold. He waits until the arena is clear, his horse is standing properly in the chute, and then he calls for him.

The first move is up to the horse. "I just wait for the horse," says Steve Cosca, "I don't make a move until he does.** Then I reach and spur him out, trying to get everything under control right there at the start. Then I open up and really spur."

"You have to spur, spur, spur," Larry Mahan says. "In fact, just before a ride that's what I'm telling myself. I walk around with a vision of my hand in the rigging and my feet in the right place, jerking them up to the rigging, cramming them back down over the points of the shoulder, starting all over again. I just walk around, grit my teeth, and run that vision through my mind over and over and over."

The PRCA rule book insists that the cowboy must spur the horse out—his spurs must be over the points of the horse's shoulders when its feet hit the ground on the first jump out of the chute—unless the horse balks and refuses to leave the chute. The cowboy can

then spur it as he would a normal riding horse. Once in the arena, the bareback rider finds his rhythm, spurring, his legs moving up and back like the pistons of a pump.

Bareback bronc riding seems to produce more individual stylists than any of the other rodeo events, partly because it is so wild and free. Joe Alexander has a style that is as close as anyone's could ever come to being perfect. He makes it look deceptively simple. Rusty Riddle, Paul Mayo, Clyde Vamvoras, and Sandy Kirby have a wild, exaggerated style; they sometimes seem to be almost lying on the horse's back, their legs spurring and flying. Larry Mahan, J. C. Trujillo, Jimmy Dix, and Steve Cosca all ride closer to their hands, chin tucked, trying for more control.

Cowboys developed bareback bronc riding in the arena. Typical of what one would expect from rodeo cowboys, they created a tough, challenging event that makes a man work for every point he gets. "Sometimes," Steve Cosca laments, shaking his head, "I just feel like the horse is jerking my head off the top of my shoulders, like somebody had started from the floor and come up and whacked me on the jaw."

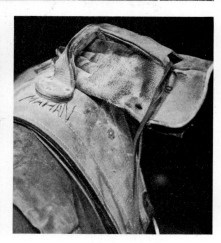

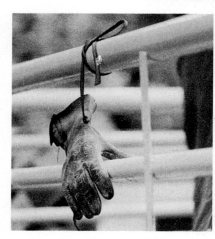

GIRLS' RODEO: BARR

EL RACING

Girls are a very big part of rodeo," declares Sammy Thurman, **professional cowgirl, member of the Girls Rodeo Association (GRA), and authority on barrel racing and training the barrel horse.** "Some of the guys like to push us back. But," she warns with a wry smile, "we might possibly be the greatest asset that the rodeo business has."

She may be right. In the last

three or four years, interest in girls' rodeo has skyrocketed. "All of a sudden," she continues, "with the women's lib bit, everything happens. They want to see women involved in everything—it doesn't make any difference what it is. Actually, the GRA didn't go out and promote itself. We didn't try to get people to have all-girl rodeos. We just kind of sat back and they came to us."

The statistics are staggering. In 1970 there were just over two hundred members in the GRA; today membership has increased four times. And since 1973, when there were thirteen all-girl rodeos in the United States, the number has escalated to almost a hundred.

Women are not new to rodeo. They have been involved in the sport since the beginning of the century. There have been women bronc riders, bull riders, steer wrestlers, and women ropers. Bertha Blancett, Nettie Hawn, Prairie Rose Smith, Alice Greenough, Fox Hastings, Fanny Sperry Steele, and Tillie Baldwin are familiar names to old rodeo buffs. They were wild and they were tough. But just exactly what they were to rodeo, was never very definite; their place in the sport was never secure. At best, women have always been regarded as something of a spectacle. You watched them because they were different, bizarre, and not because they were a significant part of any rodeo contest.

For some time women have been trying to overcome the image of being merely a freak attraction. But rodeo is a way of life and not simply another work situation; it has come out of a long, rigid cowboy tradition that includes a specific way of looking at women. Cowboys tend to be old-fashioned and courtly, and they tend to regard women as the fair—and weaker?—sex. To see women come out on a bronc or bull that they themselves might be riding ruffles that cowboy gentility. When I asked one bronc rider how he'd feel about contesting with a woman, he sighed and said: "It's not that I don't think they're strong. I see girls everyday I know could wrestle down an elephant. But that doesn't make it right. I don't want a woman to just stay in the kitchen all day, you know. But there ought to be a limit. I can't stand the idea of watching one go out in the arena and get stomped. I guess I don't want to have to watch them be <u>that</u> equal."

104

Getting girls into men's rodeo is difficult for a lot of reasons. The girls know this. As one cowgirl admits, "There is no living way you can put girls on anything that compares even closely with the stock the guys ride. The only way to make it humane, so to speak, would be to go with the superlight stock for the girls and the heavy stock for the men. Which is no contest. The girls would look better than the guys. And that would give a bad impression."

At the present time the only way to combine men and women in rodeo is to keep their events separate. The PRCA has been reluctant to approve any girls' events except the barrel racing in their rodeos. Even for that the girls have had to fight. "We do everything in our power—we push, pull, plead, get down on our knees and beg—to get barrel races at every PRCA rodeo." Some stock contractors and producers, recognizing the commercial potential of adding other all-girl contests, have attempted to get them approved. But so far the PRCA board has turned them all down.

Grudgingly, the cowboys have allowed barrel racing to become a part of their rodeos. Some of them still object to it, saying it is boring, a waste of time. But the truth is, barrel racing is a close, exciting event and beautiful to watch. As a contest it is fast and exacting; it takes a well-trained horse and a skillful rider with exceptional horse sense.

The number-one thing about barrel racing," claims Sammy Thurman, "is having a horse with speed. If a horse has got ultimate speed and all the other qualifications, he's unbeatable. Not only has a horse got to have speed, he's got to have agility; he's got to be able to handle himself in turns; and he's got to have the desire to do it. A desire above all else. You can take a horse with desire but with less of the other qualities and he can be a winner."

A description of the contest is simple: A rider, crossing the starting line at a run, makes a cloverleaf path around three barrels without knocking any of them over (she's penalized 5 seconds for each barrel she upsets—in a close contest enough to keep her from placing at all) and then races back across the finish line.

The main demand on a barrel racer is knowing how to judge the conditions of an arena and then ride her horse in such a way that she can trim every last one-hundredth of a second from her final time. The greatest barrel racers have developed a style of riding which includes subtle rein-handling techniques and leg cues designed to combine control with ultimate freedom of movement. The response is so critical that it sometimes seems these horses know exactly what their riders are thinking.

STEER

RESTLING

Steer wrestling combines
the speed and precision of calf
roping with some of the dangerous aspects of the bucking chute
events. Originally, it was called
bulldogging. A black man named
Bill Pickett is credited historically
with having started the practice of
leaping from his horse onto the
horns of a steer, bringing it to a
stop, and then biting its lip in order
to distract it enough so he could

twist it to the ground.

Doggers, as steer wrestlers are still called, look different from most rodeo cowboys. They are generally bigger, taller, and heavier. The combination of weight, strength, and agility can be important to wrestling a steer down in only a few seconds. However, size and weight don't always count. Tom Ferguson, the 1974 World Champion All-Around Cowboy, and Phil Lyne, are not big men and they've both done well in steer wrestling. They have each been able to develop techniques that help them offset the disadvantage of their size and weight. Phil, the smaller of the two men by a few inches and a few pounds, says, "As small as I am, I like to drop as much of my weight on the steer's head as possible." Which he does by waiting just a little longer than most doggers to leave his horse. He catches the steer close, gets a good hold on its horns, and really digs his heels into the dirt, which bows the steer's neck around and takes away much of its power and makes him easier to twist down.

A lot of things have to come together very fast in the steer wrestling before the cowboy can make his jump. There are two horses, two men, a steer, and a stopwatch. The steer wrestler rides one horse, his hazer the other. The job of the hazer is to keep the steer running straight and close to the steer wrestler's horse. "The role of the hazer is very important,"

declares veteran steer wrestler Frank Shepperson. "He has to read what the steer is going to do all the way and know where the steer wrestler is all the time. He cannot come out of the box too soon or he might cause the steer to stop. He has to know exactly what to do."

As in calf roping, the horse plays a vital role in the steer wrestling. The quarter horse, fast on takeoff and compact in size, is the ideal mount for the dogger. The horse must be well-trained and absolutely dependable. One skittish movement by the horse while the rider is slipping down to make his jump could cost the man his life. "Most people in the audience don't

know what is involved between the horse and the man," Frank Shepperson explains. "You've trained the horse to respond to certain cues. He carries you to the steer and then goes past the steer. But you have to guide him. You have to do that second nature. Because if you have to stop and think about guiding your horse, you'll take your mind off what you ought to be doing with the steer and you'll find yourself scooping up a mouthful of dirt."

The cattle used in this event are tall, lanky Mexican steers with sharp upcurved horns. They weigh from 450 pounds to 700 pounds. They are noted for the sinewy qualities of their bodies and their ability to run fast. As with the calf-roping stock, each steer is assigned a number, the numbers are drawn from a hat just prior to the rodeo performance, and the numbers are matched up with the cowboys who will be wrestling that day. The cowboys back their horses into a chute on either side of the chute where the steer is being held and a barrier is put up. The steer is given a head start, the barrier is jerked out of the way, and the contest begins.

The key to winning in the steer wrestling contest is being able to anticipate the right moment, recognize it, make a split-second decision, get down onto the steer, and throw him to the ground. Both horses must be running right; the steer must have its head up and be running straight. The steer wrestler will already be leaning out of the saddle. He will slip along smoothly just above the back of the steer, take a firm grip on its horns, swing completely out of the saddle, and—using his feet and legs like a set of brakes—bring the steer to a stop. While this is happening both the hazer and the steer wrestler's horse must continue to move ahead, out of the way of the cowboy and the steer. As soon as he has slowed the steer to a stop, he twists it to the ground, using the tip of the right horn and the steer's jaw as leverage. The steer must fall flat on its side with all four feet sticking out in the same direction before the run is complete and the clock stopped.

The hazards in this event are multitudinous. The first is obvious: leaping from the back of a running horse onto the head of a running steer armed with needle-

sharp horns. **"My father had a horn run completely through him,"** remembers **Frank Shepperson.** "I've seen people have their spleens and a lot of other organs punctured with horns. It just takes a slip—anything can go wrong. The steer can slip and come down on you." Once in a while a cowboy will catch his foot in a stirrup and he'll find himself caught between a horse trained to race automatically on ahead and a steer setting up to stop. A steer can step on a cowboy. It can flip over while still running and drive a horn through him or crush him under the weight of its body. But probably the most common kind of injury is to the dogger's legs. The cowboy and the steer are moving at a tremendous speed when he swings away from the horse. He braces his legs in front of him and the shock is all telescoped up through his ankles, knees and hips.

118

LL RIDING

That the average man who rides bulls weighs about 145 pounds and that the average bull weighs over 1500 pounds and has in its nature a certain treacherous streak that teaches him to turn on the man is all you need to know for a basic understanding of bull riding. For this same reason, bull riders seem to stand apart from the general run of rodeo cowboys. Theirs is the most dangerous event

A horse in the other events will try to avoid a man; a bull will not.

Proportionately, a bull may be the fastest animal alive (at least it sometimes seems so in the arena). Traditionally, he has little love for the cowboy trying to ride him. So why do cowboys do it? Why does anyone want to get on an animal that would just as soon stomp and gore him to death as not?

Bull riders hear this question a lot. They just shrug it off. Gary Leffew, 1970 World Champion Bull Rider, looks at bull riding as a challenge. "One of the things that makes bull riding appealing is the element of danger. A lot of guys get hurt. One of the things that drew me to it is that when you get one of those real bad ones that tries to get you down on his head or goes to hunting you and hooking...it starts something happening in your stomach; it's just a grinding in you. And you become tense and you worry. Overcoming this fear and defeating the bull is one of the things that keeps a guy going."

But it's not just a bad, rank bull that can hurt a cowboy. As Larry Mahan points out, "The rankest bull in the world can't throw you off any harder than a sorry, weak, no-bucking bull. If you make a mistake on any kind of bull he can slam you into the ground, step in the middle of your back or in the middle of your head, and it's all over."

There is only one requirement in bull riding—that the cowboy ride with one hand holding a loose rope for eight seconds. He doesn't need to spur. He <u>can</u> spur and pick up a few extra points from the judges. But spurring a bull greatly increases the cowboy's chances of getting thrown off balance, making a sloppy ride, and even bucking off.

The bull is ridden with a loose rope, which is approximately twelve feet long and is braided from a double length of half-inch manila rope. A loop formed by an adjustable bolen knot is tied in one end; to this loop the cowboy fastens one or two heavy bells, which serve both to make the bull buck harder and to provide enough weight to pull the rope from the bull after the rider has let go of it. A few feet from the loop, the rope is untwisted and the loose strands are divided and plaited into a flat-braided base into which is worked a flat-braided handle about twelve inches long. The tail—this is the final six feet of rope from the handle out to the free end—continues in the same flat-braided configuration, but it is gradually thinned and tapered until it is just less than an inch wide and ⅜ of an inch thick.

To put the rope on a bull, the cowboy simply threads the tail through the loop, which is adjusted to fit the girth of each bull. Then he pulls it tight up to the handle where it is wrapped around his hand. The rope is tied in no way. It binds and holds because of friction and the grip of the cowboy's hand. To increase the friction, the rider works rosin into the flat-braided handle and into the section of the rope's tail that wraps around his hand.

A good glove made of steerhide or goatskin is necessary in bull riding. A cowboy never uses the same glove he has for bareback bronc riding. He prepares this glove differently. He wants it to have a more supple palm. To achieve this, he will soften the palm with saddle soap and then work rosin into it. Just before the ride, he ties the glove around his wrist to prevent it from coming off.

Bull-riding spurs have the longest shanks of any used in the bucking events. They measure 2¼ to 2⅜ inches and are angled in anywhere from 7 degrees to 30 degrees. The five-point rowels are larger than bareback bronc rowels and they are fixed so they won't roll. The bull rider uses his spurs more as a means of holding himself on and maintaining his balance than for any showy display of riding style. Like the bareback rider, he doesn't want his boots to pull off so he binds them on with tight straps just above the ankles.

Some bull riders won't bother with chaps. However, most of them want the added protection in the chute (bulls can do a lot of crushing and bruising before they get into the arena), and the wild flapping of the chaps can make a ride look flashier and might even make the bull buck better.

Physically, bareback bronc riding may very well be the toughest event; but psychologically, at least, bull riding is second to nothing. Perhaps this is the reason bull riding seems to attract a different man. He is almost the outlaw of the rodeo circuit—speaking, of course, in the sense of cowboy law. Bull riders tend to be eccentric, changeable, quiet, and sometimes philosophical. They run the gamut of personality types from the flashy cowboys such as Larry Mahan, Don Gay, and the whole Mesquite, Texas, crew to the more clean-cut, private types like Jerome Robinson, Randy Magers, and Butch Kirby, and the philosophical cowboys like Gary Leffew, Brian Claypool, and George Brown.

Around the chutes before the bull riding begins, anticipation is almost a tangible force. Bull riders watch their bulls being loaded into the chutes, and work on their minds, getting themselves psyched up for the moment the chute gate opens. Each man puts his rope on his bull, fastening it so it will stay in place until he's ready to go. He works close to the bull, letting the animal know he's there, sitting or kneeling on its back, using the reality of this contact to calm the bull and as a further pump-up for himself.

Just before the ride, the cowboy gets down on the bull, has one or two men pull the slack out of his rope, and then warms up the rosin on the tail and handle by rubbing them rapidly with his gloved hand to create friction. He fits his hand into the handle, lining it up down the center of the bull's back, lays the tail of the rope across his palm, wraps it once around the back of his hand and brings it across his palm again. Sometimes a cowboy will twist this final wrap of the rope so he has additional bulk and bind when he closes his hand down on it. This is done at the final moment before going into the arena, and as one young bull rider says, "Once you run your hand in the rope and take your wrap, the main thing you want to do is just bear down and just try and just hold on for your life."

The cowboy rides holding his free arm up and moving, sort of like a counterweight to help him stay balanced. For a number of reasons, bulls are difficult to ride. They have a loose hide, and they are tricky buckers. They can come out of the chute and go into a spin, and continue to spin in one spot for much of the ride; or they can reverse the direction of the spin and reverse it again. A cowboy has to learn to hustle and shuffle, push and pull, and to scrap and monkey to keep himself in the middle of a bull's back.

There are two basic approaches to bull-riding style. One is to ride with full muscle power—that is, to hold the rope hard and stiffen the whole body to hold to and cling with the movement of the bull. A big man will often use this approach with more success than a small man. The second approach is to ride looser, to monkey up to the rope, to keep the arms and legs flexible to absorb the constant power of the shock and jerk of the bull's bucking pattern. The looser ride is less hard on the man's body and usually looks freer and classier.

One of the most unsettling things about riding bulls is that once the ride is over there is no way to the ground except to buck off. The cowboy chooses his moment, reaches and unfastens the final wrap from around his hand, and jumps, using the momentum of the peak of the bull's buck to propel him as far away as possible.

That is the ideal way to buck off. It is the one that is in the cowboy's mind as he plans out his ride. Gary Leffew and Don Gay like to see themselves jumping off and holding up their hands to the crowd for approval and applause. But it doesn't always happen as planned. The bull itself is one hazard, which doesn't need any explaining. The other is the rope, which can be a trap. Occasionally, a cowboy's hand will get hung up in the rope and the bull will sling him down and hook him and step on him. Sometimes the rope binds the cowboy's hand so badly it won't jerk free and he must then somehow pull himself to his feet, run alongside the bull, and try to get the rope loose with his free hand. Considering how fast a bull is and that he is either trying to get the man or get away from him, pulling free from a hang-up is not easy. Wrists and arms and legs are broken, ribs and skulls are caved in. Many times it is only the effort of a rodeo clown, jumping in at the right moment and undoing the rope, that saves the cowboy.

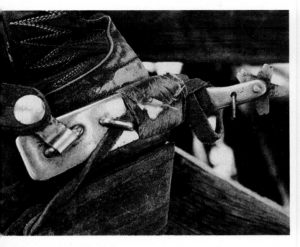

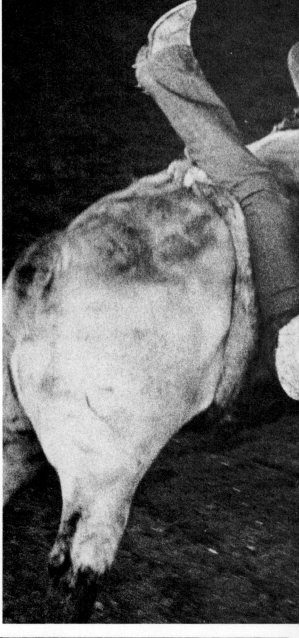

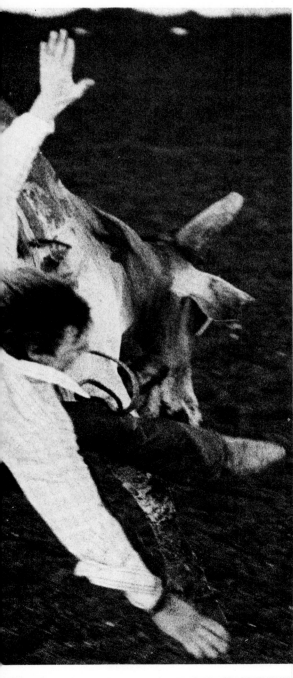

131

O CLOWNS

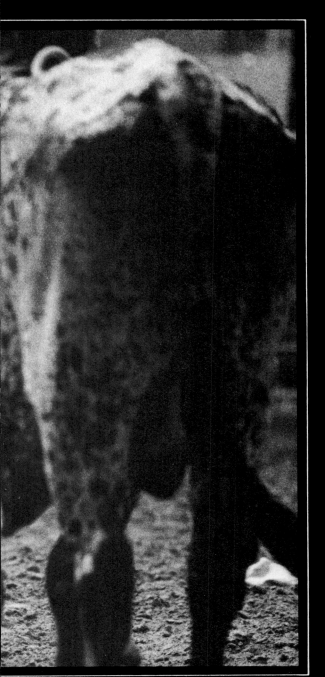

The cowboy clown is a special kind of clown. He looks funny enough, swimming around in a pair of huge overalls, big bandana handkerchiefs tied all over him like flags. And he can make you laugh—especially if you're a kid. He will have a trick car or a trained dog or monkey, a burro, bull, pony, or a pig. His pants will explode and burn. He paints his face like a harlequin and effects the worst kind of ratty wigs. He knows a handful of weary jokes touching on the baser aspects of politics and the kind of trash-can sociology that can still allow him to use hippies and women as targets. Fortunately, most of them get lost somewhere between the announcer and the bucking chutes.

But it doesn't matter. All the funny stuff is secondary to what the cowboy clown really is hired to do. Take a closer look at this man: His clothes are ridiculous-looking and they may seem cumbersome, but they're actually cut so the man can move, so he can dodge and run. He won't be wearing big flop-sole clown shoes. He'll have a runner's shoes, something with cleats, spikes, treads, the kind of shoes a quarterback would wear, or a short-stop. You won't be able to see that he has an athlete's body. But watch him: He carries himself well. And he's probably in better shape than most of the cowboys. He has to be.

The clown can play at being funny for most of the rodeo. But as soon as the bull riding starts, his work gets serious. His main task in this event is to save lives; and every bull rider who's been goin' down the road for any length of time at all can tell you it does happen. They'll also tell you a good clown can make a bull buck harder. Wick Peth is one of those clowns who not only tries to save the cowboy from injury, but also helps him make a better ride. "He'll get down on his hands and knees and just almost kiss one right on the end of the nose to get him to turn back for you," Phil Lyne says. "He has enabled me to place at rodeos where I couldn't have done a thing otherwise because he'd get a bull to buck so much better."

Wick Peth's move of getting down on his hands and knees in the path of a bucking bull would be branded by Ernest Hemingway as pure spectacle tainted with cheap-ness. Wick would defend it as being a kind of madness with a method to it. "I go flat," he says, "because when the bull goes by and he sees me and I'm standing up, he just sees my feet and he thinks, <u>Oh hell, I'll never catch him, just another one of them sorry clowns who's going to run and get on the fence</u>. But if I go down on one knee and the bull's bucking with his head down and he looks over and sees me down there, he's more apt to come around toward me."

Most rodeo clowns have been cowboys. Some of them still are. They'll continue to contest, working an event such as steer wrestling during the course of their employment at a rodeo. Whether they compete or not, they're as hooked on rodeo as the cowboys. For instance, Duane Reichart could be teaching school. "I've got a school-teaching degree. I guess moneywise I might be able to do better being a plumber or a carpenter or a schoolteacher. But I like rodeo—it's my life. There's something about making people laugh that makes me feel good. A clown's real job is taking the bulls away from the cowboys, and it's kind of hard to explain the feeling I get from that. But I can say it's good, it's what I like to do, and that's the reason I'm doing it."

The pride is there, as Carl Doering puts it: "A fellow's got to be rather versatile in this rodeo business. You've got to fight bulls and save the cowboys and also be a clown. This is different from both the Mexican bullfighter and the circus clown. And we kind of pride ourselves on being able to be this way....If you get somebody who's in real bad shape, up against a fence or in a corner, and the bull's got a horn down ready to nail him and you just step in there at the right moment—well, I'll tell you what, it makes you feel like a million dollars. There isn't money that can buy that."

The cowboys would be the first to agree. The clowns know this and, as Rick Young says, it is an added incentive to work that much harder. "What makes you feel good is when a man like Freckles Brown, Phil Lyne, or Larry Mahan comes up to you and congratulates you for helping them out in a bull ride. It makes you feel good to know they know you're out there doing the best you can and that if something happens to them it's just an accident."

A clown has to get himself psyched up for the bulls. It isn't the same as with a bull rider—who encounters only one bull at each performance. The clown has to get himself up to face from twelve to twenty bulls. Some of the old hands get pumped up while putting on their makeup in a camper or trailer and thinking about what they've got to do, what they've done a thousand times before. For some of the younger clowns it's harder. One reason is that they are taking

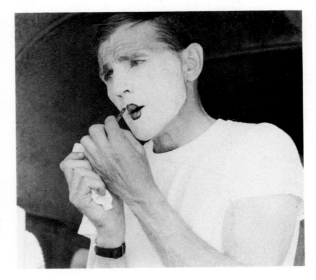

greater chances in an attempt to make a name for themselves and get more contracts for the coming year. I watched one young clown in California take his gear down into the bull pen and then sit in a corner, change clothes, and put on his paint. He just kept watching the bulls, letting them back off and snort and paw.

Sometimes a crowd can help a clown. "It's a hard thing to psych yourself into sometimes," Chuck Henson admits. "But when there's a grandstand full of people screaming and hollering and laughing and everything, it pumps you up and you can really go ahead and do something. It makes it a lot easier with a big crowd."

"And especially," Rick Young adds, "at a place like Calgary, where the people are very enthusiastic. The more enthusiasm you have, the better you're going to fight bulls, the better you're going to clown. You're naturally going to do more than you would at a place where everybody sits there like you're a dummy or something. Where there's a lot of people and

they're doing a lot of hollering and screaming—well, by gosh, you're liable to do anything."

Almost anything. Wick Peth claims: "I never take chances. I'm thinking about my body. When I first started clowning I went seven or eight years and never got hurt seriously. I always thought, Well, hell, I can't be hurt." Wick doesn't smile a lot. But when he does now, there is a tracing of gold repair work along his teeth. "But I found out later that I'm just like anybody else."

Clowning and bull fighting is dangerous business. And clowns do get hurt. How? Carelessness, for one thing. And failure to recognize the depth of intelligence in bulls. Carl Doering knows about bulls. "If you set a trap for a bull, you can bet he's going to

gather you sooner or later....Like Joe Louis said: 'You can run but you can't hide.'"

"A lot of old, smart bulls," Wick Peth says, "will stand there and watch you turn. They're waiting for me to make a mistake or get a little too close. I might do the same thing to a bull three or four times and he'll just kind of watch me. Then, someday, at some performance, he'll jump and catch me...."

A cowboy, if he's got a wife, can't always take her down the road with him. If he's making enough money to afford it then he's probably moving much too fast to be able to see her anyway. A clown is different. He goes to a rodeo and stays there until it is over—two days, a week, ten days. So often he will take his family. Chuck Henson maintains it's a great life. "You can travel and see all of the country. You're making good money and you can enjoy yourself. I have a house trailer and I take my wife, Nancy, and my two little girls, Nancy Jane and Annie. We stop off and go fishing and hunting. We visit our friends around the country and sightsee a lot. I try to take my kids to all the places I saw when I was a kid. It's pretty educational for them. It's just a good life, it really is."

It is if the clown's wife will accept the kind of work her husband has to do. Nancy Henson figured that out many years ago. "Chuck was doing it when we married, and I made up my mind a long time before we ever got married that I wasn't going to worry about it...that we'd take it one day at a time. And it's paid off."

Or as Johnny Wilson's wife puts it: "I know he's a good clown and very athletic. And I know from years of experience that if he gets hooked or gets hurt and it's not an accident, if he didn't slip and fall in front of the bull and the bull ran over him, he deserves every pain he feels. I don't fall apart like many cowboys' wives do. Not anymore. Three years ago, when I first met him, I did. But not anymore. It doesn't pay. Besides, somebody's got to keep cool about the whole thing and take care of business."

144

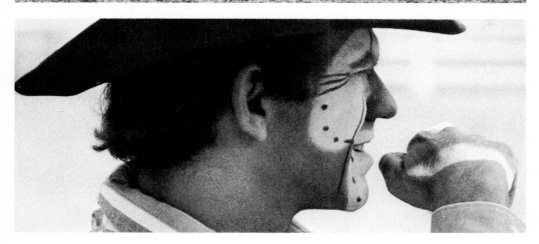

TAKING UP

HE SLACK

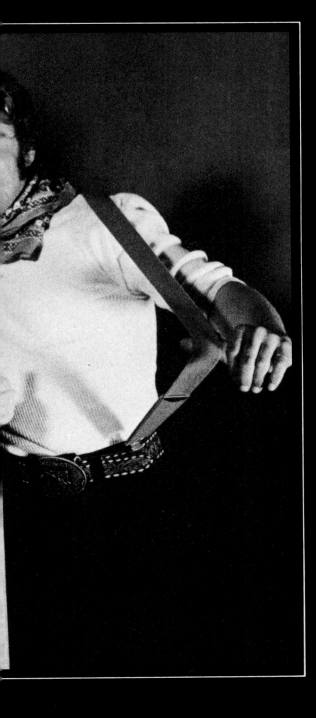

Even the toughest competitors don't beat themselves up and down the road all the time. There are certain slack periods at the big fall and winter rodeos when they spend whole days and nights in one town. Then the cowboy life can get pretty loose. Cowboys take over entire hotels and motels in San Francisco, Denver, Fort Worth, Houston, and Phoenix. They gather at night for

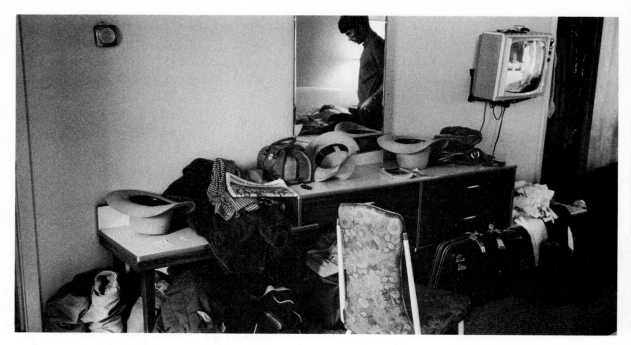

parties that flow from room to room, from day to day. Guitars appear. Mel Hyland has been traveling with his guitar for years. Don Gay takes his guitar down the road when he can find room for it. Cowboys pick and sing and trade tunes. Bareback rider Chris LeDoux usually has a new song. Bull rider Don Graham sings. And Monty Henson has hinted that after his rodeo career he might try making it as a country singer.

San Francisco is the first big slowdown after the long summer season. The cowboys suddenly find themselves with whole days and nights of no place to go and no stock to ride. They make the most of it. After the rodeo performance at the Cow Palace last October 29, the cowboys and spectators gathered to witness the Cowboy World Championship Heavyweight Boxing Match. A few preliminary lightweight bouts were fought between bull riders and bronc riders; they came out in bare feet and jeans and battered at each other until they had to be hauled back into their corners and cooled down for the next round. The main attraction of the evening was the match between the notorious Allen "Killer" Keller, a steer roper from Olathe, Colorado, and Jimmy Nickerson, sometime cowboy and movie double for the rodeo cowboy-actor James Caan. They fought ten hard close rounds, with Keller finally winning by a decision.

Two nights later, cowboys in outrageous costumes took over Fisherman's Wharf, where Gary Leffew was holding his annual Buckin' Ball. Larry Mahan showed up as an aging hooker with an illegitimate son named "Linda" in tow. Don Graham, Monty Henson, and Don Gay came as DA'd Fifties greaseballs. There were pumpkins (Leffew's pregnant wife), perverts, cops, and a nun. Typical of rodeo blowouts, it was long and wild; and as morning approached, the cowboys were doing their best to try and stomp the sun back into the sea.

It is not always peaceful. There are notorious cowboy bashes, wild drunken nights in rodeo towns that have ended in fights with everything from spurs to belt buckles and broken beer bot-

tles and occasionally even knives, brawls ugly enough to rival any old frontier tale of the boys in town for a night of just plain raising hell. Rodeo does have its troublemakers and thugs. But there aren't many, and the majority of the cowboys don't want to be involved with them.

Most cowboys are not above a good prank, however, especially if they're playing it on another cowboy, preferably a good friend and traveling companion. The road, all those hours in a car, driving, sitting, can be pretty boring. Even an inexhaustible supply of eight-track cartridges, isometrics, and magazine centerfolds can't dampen some cowboys' ruthlessly imaginative attempts at finding a sore spot in a friend. Dennis Holland, a bull rider and ex-prizefighter from Oakland,

California, remembers a story that easily outdistances simple short-sheetings and fire-hose baptisms:

"One time I was traveling with Gary Leffew and some other guys. I was driving. Everybody started getting hungry. So I stopped the car and went in this place to get some hamburgers and milk shakes. I got back in and started driving. I reached over the back seat to get a hamburger and they all started getting on me about watching where I was going. Pretty soon, someone said: 'Hey, look out for that truck up ahead!' I said I saw it. About the same time, Gary Leffew nudged me and said: 'Have some of these onion rings—they're getting cold.' So I kind of reached over and got some. They felt greasy, you know. So I just stuck one in my mouth and kept on driving. But this old onion ring started crawling out of my mouth. I spit it out and looked at it: It was a worm. And everybody started just howling and laughing. I guess while I was in buying the food someone had slipped into a bait shop next door there and bought this bunch of big fishing worms."

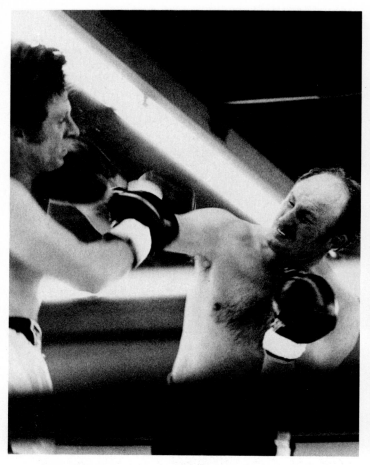

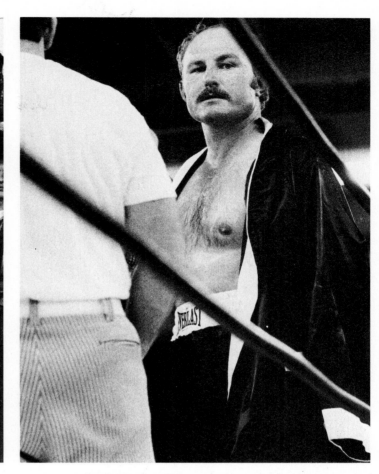

151

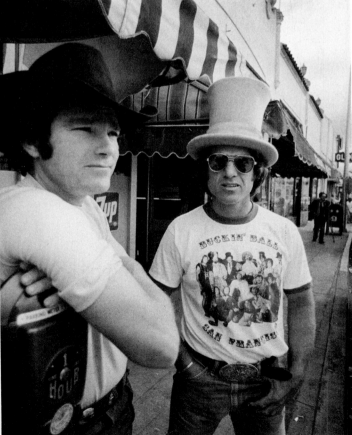

AFTER-WORD

RODEO—AMERICA'S NUMBER-
ONE SPORT." You see the words all across the country—on the sides of
buildings, on bumper stickers, on T-shirts...But is it really America's
number-one sport? The cowboys believe it is, and there is a lot to recommend it for that title. At a time when many professional sports have turned
into big business and the pitfalls of that world have left them in such a
desperate state that their very lives depend almost totally on the support of
TV sponsorship, rodeo continues to be independent, to grow and to thrive.
Rodeo's high level of sportsmanship, the lure of the ultimate gamble, and
the promise of a life of almost total freedom from the stifling clutches of
regular employment and the rigid structure of team play set it apart from
most other sports.

But rodeo is more than a sport, more than a test of skill and stamina. It has become a way of life for a unique breed of human being that once seemed threatened with extinction. And if we were seeking a symbol to stand for America, a

man who might sum up its spirit and worth, who might reflect its qualities of determination, free enterprise, and forthrightness, we could easily find it in one kind of man—the cowboy.

A GUIDE TO IDENTIFICATION
OF CONTESTANTS, CLOWNS, AND JUDGES

The author offers apologies to those contestants, clowns, judges, and other persons whom he has been unable to identify. He welcomes any identifications of those he has missed, and will hopefully incorporate that information in the next printing.

Page numbers in italic in the following list indicate an appearance of that person in the *unnumbered* eight-page color insert following page 48.